HISTORY OF

San Diego Rotary
2001–2011

THE CENTENNIAL

by Deborah Cox Mandabach

Dedication

To my late parents, Janice and Dyson Cox,

who instilled in me the joys of reading and writing almost from day one;

and

to my husband, Fred,

who has been through it all with me, and makes everything more fun!

THE
DONNING COMPANY
PUBLISHERS

The Donning Company Publishers
184 Business Park Drive, Suite 206
Virginia Beach, VA 23462

Steve Mull, *General Manager*
Barbara Buchanan, *Office Manager*
Heather L. Floyd, *Editor*
Stephanie Danko, *Graphic Designer*
Priscilla Odango, *Imaging Artist*
Steve Hartman, *Project Research Coordinator*
Tonya Washam, *Marketing Specialist*
Pamela Engelhard, *Marketing Advisor*

Dwight Tompkins, *Project Director*

Library of Congress Cataloging-in-Publication Data

Mandabach, Deborah Cox
    History of San Diego Rotary, 2001–2011 : the centennial / by Deborah Cox Mandabach.
        p. cm.
    Includes index.
    ISBN 978-1-57864-759-0 (hbk. : alk. paper)
 1. San Diego Rotary Club 33—History. I. Title.
    HF5001.R82S286 2012
    369.5'209794985—dc23

                        2012011569

Printed in the United States of America at Walsworth Publishing Company

Table of Contents

Acknowledgments

The phrase "We stand on the shoulders of those who have gone before" could not be more accurate. This, the fourth volume of the history of the San Diego Rotary, is not the work of just one person or one group. Hundreds of people have contributed to our history, dating all the way back to the founding of Club 33 in 1911.

Grateful thanks go to the members of the History Committees throughout Club 33's one-hundred-year history. They, along with others, had the vision and desire to commit to permanent memory the history of a legendary organization. What a gift to the community!

The main resource for compiling this volume was the *Rotator*, 520 issues edited by twenty-eight different Rotarians. The average number of *Rotator*s edited by each person would be eighteen; however, three members edited the most issues: Steve Hubbard (forty-five), Larry Clapper (forty-two), and Hugh Carter (thirty-nine and a half). It should be noted that Hugh edged out Richard Ledford (thirty-nine), who in turn edged out Geri Warnke (thirty-eight and a half), due to the fact that she and Hugh shared editing duties for one issue.

Had it not been for the *Rotator*s, interviews with the nine living past presidents, and other members willing to answer questions and share their stories and memories, this project would have been Herculean, if not impossible, and not nearly as much fun as it actually was.

Without the photographic talents of Burt Nestor, Paul Nestor, and Mike Conner, as well as many others who selflessly contributed time and photographic prowess, there would be no photos. We owe a special debt of gratitude to each of them.

Extra special thanks are due to an extraordinary staff who helped me with everything: Executive Director Bruce Hunt shepherded the project from day one, and Executive Assistant Pauline Hill tracked down facts, identified people in photos, and graciously answered a million questions throughout this entire process.

On a personal note, I want to thank a cadre of special friends (you know who you are), my new friends in Rotary, and business colleagues who—with encouragement and assurances—said again and again that this project would actually get done. You were right!

Deborah Cox Mandabach
San Diego, California
June 2012

Introduction

Welcome to the fourth volume of the one-hundred-year history of the San Diego Rotary Club celebrating one hundred years of service in the San Diego region.

The first and second volumes of the history of the San Diego Rotary Club, which cover 1911 to 1991, were researched and written by the late Rear Admiral Joseph L. Howard, a much-beloved and highly respected member of the community. Volume three (1991–2001) was written by multi-talented writer Joanne R. Gribble, PhD. Without those volumes, the task would have been nearly impossible and certainly would have taken vastly longer than the eighteen months scheduled.

The San Diego Rotary Club has a deep and rich history, much of which is interwoven with the city of San Diego itself. Since the early days of San Diego, many prominent people have held leadership positions in Club 33 and have influenced the business, educational, and military life of the region. Founders such as Barbour, Brockett, Cleator, Davies, Frost, Heilbron, Kettner, Jessop, and others were a vibrant part of San Diego. Generations of those families continue to be actively involved in the life of both San Diego and the San Diego Rotary Club.

A Decade of Transitions

This volume covers the first decade of a new century, from July 1, 2001 to June 30, 2011, or as I call it, "a decade of transitions." Significant changes occurred during this time, including upgrading and refurbishing the office, hiring a new executive director, updating and formalizing financial policies and operational procedures, and revising the by-laws, which had been unchanged since 1911. The adoption of new technology resulted in online services and more efficient communications. In 2001, Facebook, PayPal, LinkedIn, eBay, and Wikipedia did not exist. Today, those websites are part of the daily lives of Rotarians as well as millions of users worldwide. Google, Kindle, Twitter, and YouTube didn't exist in 2001. Today, those words are part of our daily vocabulary.

There were several significant "bookends" in this decade. Apple introduced the iPod in 2001, and by June 2011, there were 225 million active users. In between, the iPhone and iPad were introduced to instant popularity.

The worst terrorist attack on U.S. soil in history occurred on September 11, 2001, and on May 1, 2011, Osama Bin Laden, widely acknowledged as the architect of the attack, was captured, killed, and buried at sea.

And, on a more entertaining note, Harry Potter was born in 2001 and "retired" in 2011 after ten years of a very public—and successful—life.

All in all, this decade was "one for the books!"

CHAPTER ONE

Paul J. Hartley, Jr.

2001–2002

" If it can't be played on the ukulele, it's not worth singing! "

▲ **ASK ANYONE WHAT THEY THINK OF WHEN THEY THINK OF PAUL HARTLEY, JR.,** and several things come to mind: his outlandish sports jackets, his undying loyalty to the U.S. Navy, his much-loved "tomatoes," his complete dedication and devotion to all things Rotary, and, of course, his ever-present ukulele.

CHANGE OF COMMAND

The July 5 "Change of Command" ceremony of President Paul Hartley, Jr. could not have been more appropriate for Club 33's retired Navy captain. Not to disappoint the fashion-conscious in the crowd, Hartley wore one of his many signature plaid sports jackets. Mayor (and fellow Rotarian) Dick Murphy judiciously led the swearing-in of President Hartley and the new Board of Directors. Hartley introduced his wife and favorite "tomato," Charlotte; his daughters, Janet, Pamela, and Sarah; his son, Paul; and the 2001–2002 board members. He closed his very first meeting by urging all Rotarians to proudly wear their pins every day, and then fined the *absent* Dick Knoth for not wearing his. During the year, hardly a Club 33 member escaped the clutches of President Hartley and his fearless fine pattern.

Plans for the Year

Plans for the new year included "Global Quest," the Rotary International theme which emphasized growth in membership. As a result, forty-six new members joined—eight over the goal—bringing Club 33's membership to 550 members, the sixth-largest club in the world at that time.

Several new committees were established, including a Strategic Planning Committee.

Led by Stan Hartman, it was charged with the task of revising the constitution and by-laws, which had not been done since the founding of Club 33 in 1911. Fundraising was formalized with emphasis placed on increasing member donations and fines. Toward the end of his command, Hartley was asked, "Why do you feel the need to seek out the weak and throw them asunder?" The former naval captain's response was "I fine 'em 'cause I can't throw 'em in the brig!"

A first in the Paul Hartley, Jr. term was the establishment of a Past Presidents Club, which afforded past presidents the opportunity to get together more formally for both social and club-related occasions. He also began the custom of inviting input from all the past presidents at the beginning of a presidential term.

Club 33's 90th Anniversary

The 90th Anniversary Gala was held on February 7, 2002, at the Sheraton East Grand Ballroom. Over 400 Rotarians and guests attended the event chaired by Jim Hughes and Patti Roscoe. One of Club 33's gifts to the city was in the form of ninety new volunteers who were slated to provide service in the areas where school partners are located, including Sherman Elementary, Wilson Middle School, and Hoover, San Diego, and Monarch high schools.

Evening highlights included former San Diego mayor and governor Pete Wilson, who talked about what the Rotary meant to San Diego during his two terms as mayor. A video created by Mark Trotter, John Eger, and Philippe Lamoise added a special touch, and kudos were lavished on event chairs Jim Hughes and Patti Roscoe. In an update letter to the membership, Hartley described the evening of remembering the past, appreciating the present, and looking to the future. He stated, "I plan on being around for the one-hundredth just to see if it can match the ninetieth!" Sadly, this was not to be, as the beloved Paul Hartley, Jr. passed away on August 23, 2008.

▲ Top: *Mayor Dick Murphy presented President Paul Hartley with a City of San Diego proclamation honoring Club 33's 90th Anniversary.*

▲ Top middle: *Former mayor and governor Pete Wilson, Patti Roscoe, and Mayor Dick Murphy at the 90th Anniversary celebration.*

▲ Bottom middle: *Nancy Scott and Diana Venable shared a toast at the 90th Anniversary meeting.*

▲ Bottom: *George Gildred (left) and Art Rivkin enjoyed the 90th Anniversary meeting.*

The World Pauses in the Wake of Tragedy

One of the defining moments—and certainly the most tragic—of the decade was September 11, 2001. As most people were preparing for their day, the world was changing in unimaginable ways. The massive terrorist attacks that occurred in New York City, Washington, D.C., and Shanksville, Pennsylvania, brought daily activities to a complete halt across the entire country.

The September 13 meeting of Club 33 was somber. President Hartley called for a silent prayer for the victims of the tragedy and their families. Greg Zinser led the group in singing "God Bless America," and in her invocation, Gloria Harris quoted George Washington's call for courage and God's help. City Manager Michael Uberuaga shared his personal feelings about the unspeakable acts of terrorism that took so many innocent lives and described his son's experience and safe evacuation from the American Express building near the Twin Towers.

John Rebelo later reported on his experience in Washington, D.C., on September 11. "We left a meeting around 9:00 a.m. to head over to the hill for our scheduled meetings and noticed a very large crowd around the television. Pictures were flashing regarding what was taking place in New York City and right at that time the Pentagon was hit. Our hotel, just above the Pentagon, was less than one mile away. Police directed everyone away from the area as it was anticipated that the Capitol would be the next target."

Along with other colleagues from the West Coast, John spent days trying to get a flight home. When it became apparent that flights out of Washington, D.C., were not happening, they rented a car, drove to Omaha, and, thanks to Holiday Bowl sponsor Frontier Airlines, were able to catch a flight home to San Diego. There were only six passengers on that flight.

SERVICE ABOVE SELF

Plans to integrate and re-emphasize service opportunities into Club 33 life included programs such as Avoidable Blindness, Village Banking, Jobs for the Disabled, organ donation sign-ups, senior services, and scouting and family activities. Although Mercy Day, scheduled for September 15, had to be cancelled due to 9/11, other club projects were carried out as planned. The Malawi Wheelchair Project continued, the World Community Service Days Committee was praised for ongoing work across the border, and the Fish Across the Border Project resulted in 137 cases of tuna and $2,500 toward filling grocery bags.

November 29 was the dedication of Monarch High School, which was founded in 1987 by Sandra McBrayer as the PLACE (Progressive Learning Alternative for Children's Education), San Diego's public school for homeless children. The library was named the Rotary Club Board of Directors Room, and the computer room was named for Rotarian Peter Van Horne and his wife, Dee. It was observed that since Monarch School's move from Market Street, enrollment had doubled to 120 and dual class sessions were being considered.

Rotary does service in Tijuana and Tecate, Mexico, on a monthly basis. That year, April 6 was Rotary Service Day in Tijuana.

MEMBERSHIP

Fellowship, Camaraderie, and Engagement

There's Always Time for Fun!

An important part of life as a Rotarian is the opportunity for fellowship and fun. Kicking off the fun for the year was the annual "Day at the Races," held on August 15 and attended by forty Rotarians and guests. Although there were no big winners, a ton of fun was had by all! Other events during the year included the annual Sail and BBQ at the San Diego Yacht Club in September, golf outings in October and June, and a ski trip to Whistler, British Columbia, Canada, in March.

In the intraclub golf competition, Bob Jacobs, the 2001–2002 overall champion, won the coveted Jack Thompson Memorial Trophy. Other stars included individual event low gross winners Don Tartre and Peter Platt and low net winners Bruce Blakley and Hal Gardner. In the women's division, the low gross winner was Bonnie Schwartz, and the low net winners were Kay North and Lisa Miller. Long drive big hitters were Tom Wilson, Peter Platt, and Bob Jacobs. Closest to the pin awards went to Vance Gustafson, Tom Creamer, Rick Richards, Don Tartre, and Bob Mattis.

Member News

Club 33 members are notoriously generous with their time; not only for Rotary activities and projects, but for many other San Diego organizations as well. Mike Murphy co-chaired the American Cancer Society's Corporate Council of Hope for 2001–2002. Joyce Gattas chaired the San Diego Art Institute's 45th Annual International Awards Exhibition. Katherine Kennedy co-chaired the Globe Theater's "Snow-Globe" event. Phil Klauber co-chaired a party at the Museum of Photographic Arts

Camp Enterprise, April 11–13, 2002

The chair for Camp Enterprise was Dave Sapper. Pronounced by many to be "The Best Ever Camp Enterprise," Rotarians heard from keynote speaker and baseball legend/future Hall-of-Famer Tony Gwynn at the luncheon meeting. His positive frame of mind rubbed off on the students and they headed for camp with great expectations. The winning project was Beachside Bagels, whose facilitators were Claudia Johnson and Dennis Humberstone.

Judges were past Camp Enterprise chairs Berit Durler, Jack Carpenter, and Kirk Jackson.

▲ Tony Gwynn was the keynote speaker at the Camp Enterprise kick-off meeting.

honoring Audrey Geisel. The 2002 Super Bowl Host Committee included President Ky Snyder and Reint Reinders, the Hospitality co-chair. In addition, Patti Roscoe handled special events and John Hawkins managed the volunteers' efforts.

Awards and Honors

Throughout the year, many Rotarians received honors and awards from local and regional agencies. Homer D. Peabody, Jr., MD and his wife, Betty, were the first recipients of the Millennium Award granted by the Balboa Park Millennium Society. Jerry Sanders and Lucy Killea served as honorary chairs. Phil Klauber received a George W. Marston Award for Civic Leadership at the San Diego Historical Society's inaugural History Makers Dinner. Laurie Black, Patti Roscoe, and Cheryl Wilson were named "Women of Dedication" by the Salvation Army Women's Auxiliary. Darlene Davies received the 2002 Mortar Board Distinguished Alumna Award from the Mortar Board Alumni Chapter of San Diego County. Bob Arnhym was named to the Miss America Academy of Honor. Paul Tchang was inducted into the California Building Industry Hall of Fame, and the Corporate Directors Forum honored Rich Collato as a "Director of the Year." Malin Burnham was honored with the Chancellor's Medal by UCSD for "extraordinary contributions to education and the greater San Diego Community." Judy McDonald received the 2002 Morgan Award, named for author and *Union Tribune* columnist Neil Morgan, for twenty-five years of service to the San Diego community from LEAD San Diego. San

Diego land economics society Lambda Alpha International presented the Annual Recognition Award to Roy Potter and his wife, Ruth. Janie Davis, Katherine Kennedy, and Mary Walshok were nominated by the National Association of Women Business Owners (NAWBO) for BRAVO! Awards. Bonnie Schwartz was named winner of the BRAVO! "Woman Business Owner of the Year" award. Bill Gore was honored by the University of San Diego with an Author E. Hughes Career Achievement Award from the College of Arts & Sciences. This award, established in 1995, is named in honor of University of San Diego President Emeritus Author E. Hughes. Mary Walshok received the Royal Order of the Polar Star by the consul general of Sweden.

In other news, Cecil Steppe was named president of the San Diego Urban League. John Hawkins was named chair of the San Diego Convention & Visitors Bureau. John Chane was elected bishop of the Episcopal Diocese of Washington, D.C. The San Diego Press Club named John Hawkins "Entrepreneur Headliner," and Bill Gore was named "Law Enforcement Headliner."

Maurie Watson and his wife, Jacqueline, provided a grant to The San Diego Foundation which was used to commission well-known artist James Hubbell to create a life sculpture, "Water Spirit," for placement at the end of Shelter Island.

Significant birthdays were celebrated by Dick Clark, who turned ninety-seven, Ferd Fletcher, ninety-one, and Art Jacobs, ninety. Join Rotary and live a long and productive life!

New Members

NAME	PRIMARY SPONSOR
Ray Ashley, Maritime Museum Association of San Diego	Ken Andersen
Catherine Anderson, San Diego Film Commission	Joyce Gattas
David Bejarano, San Diego Police Department	Jerry Sanders
Deborah Berger, Office of the San Diego City Attorney	Lucy Killea
Javed Bhaghani, Tom James Co.	Joe Farrage
Karen Bishop, EdD, Futures International High School	Yvonne Murchison
Thella Bowens, San Diego International Airport	Sandy Purdon
Barbara Bry, Proflowers	Martha Dennis
Dick Davis, Kyoto Symposium Organization	Allan Boothe
Bishop Roy Dixon, Faith Chapel Church of God in Christ	Patti Roscoe
Steven Escoboza, Healthcare Association of San Diego and Imperial Counties	Nikki Clay
Daryl E. Ferguson, Management Consultant	Paul J. Hartley, Jr.
William G. Fiss, William G. Fiss & Associates	Sandy Purdon
Beverly Frischner, BBF Associates	Joanne Pastula
Veronica "Ronne" Froman, San Diego Unified School District	Nikki Clay
James M. Frost, Frost Hardware Lumber Co.	G. T. Frost
Thomas S. Gehring, San Diego County Medical Society	Dave Knetzer
Joyce Glazer, Community Volunteer	Frank Arrington
Patrick Goddard, Jr., Nethere, Inc.	Pat Goddard
Michael Hager, Natural History Museum	Pat Crowell
Laura Spitler Hansen, Age Concerns, Inc.	B. J. Spitler
Craig Irving, Confirmnet Corp.	Ray Robbins
James H. Jackson, Jr., San Diego Rescue Mission	Mark Trotter
Edward W. Kitrosser, Turnquist, Schmitt, Kitrosser & McMahon	Bruce Blakley
Bob Kyle, Dearborn Publishing (Ret.)	Fred Frye
Sandra L. Mayberry, Esq.	Chet Lathrop
Bill McCloskey, Allison McCloskey Escrow Co.	Steve Cairncross
Ray McKewon, Accredited Home Lenders, Inc.	Roy Potter
Eugene Mitchell, San Diego Regional Chamber of Commerce	Joe Craver
Linda Moore, Linda Moore Gallery/Linda Moore Fine Arts	Marie Huff
Vincent Mudd, San Diego Office Interiors	Joe DeCristofaro
Daniel E. Murphy II, Barney & Barney (Ret.)	Marie Huff
Joe Murphy, CB Richard Ellis	Michelle Candland
Robert Noble, Tucker Sadler Noble Castro	Hal Sadler
Joe Outlaw, Pen Trust Financial Services	Jack Thompson
Joseph Panetta, BIOCOM/San Diego	Mary Colacicco
Ian Pumpian, PhD, San Diego State University	Steve Weber
Vivian Reznik, MD, UCSD School of Medicine	Cindy Olmstead

(continued on next page)

(continued from previous page)

NAME	PRIMARY SPONSOR
Steve Rice, U.S. Bank	John Zygowicz
John P. Sands, Jr., MD (Ret.)	Paul J. Hartley, Jr.
Rob Schlesinger, Zoological Society of San Diego	Doug Myers
Jim Standiford, First United Methodist Church of San Diego	George Jessop
Linda Stirling, Merrill Lynch	Quint Ellis
William L. White, The Ascot Shop	Will Newbern
Bob Witty, San Diego Historical Society	Pat Crowell
Joe Zakowski, DDS	Carol Summerhays, DDS

HONORARY MEMBERS

Pauline des Granges

Rudulfo Figueroa, Consul of Mexico

Doris Howell, MD, UC San Diego (Ret.)

John Norton

Carol Whaley, San Diego High School

B. J. Williams, Mrs. San Diego, 1994

In Memoriam

Donald G. Buss

Gordon T. Frost

Clinton D. McKinnon

Admiral U.S.G. "Oley" Sharp, USN (Ret.)

Hugh D. Weckerly

Rotarian of the Month

Geri Warnke, August

Grotarian Events

Grotarian events included a July evening at the home of Nancy Scott and an April visit to the FBI office in San Diego.

Rotarians of the Quarter

Richard Weiner

Chuck Pretto

Pat Robinson

Ellen Casey

PROGRAMS

President Hartley had a unique presence at the podium and, although programs were a big draw, members admitted that they also looked forward to seeing what the president would do. To keep the program moving, he often bestowed the "I Thought I Was the Speaker" award on a long-winded introducer. It was effective—and both delivered and received all in good fun!

In true San Diego Rotary tradition, the weekly programs covered subjects from sports and entertainment to healthcare, education, and city and regional politics and back again!

Who Doesn't Love Sports in San Diego?

La Jolla resident Dick Enberg, one of America's premier television sportscasters, presented a crowd-pleasing program on July 12. The Emmy recipient shared terrific stories about his life in sports, including Wimbledon (his best event), Nolan Ryan's no-hitter at Tiger Stadium (his most exciting), and the Washington Redskins' Super Bowl game (his toughest).

Foreign/Exotic Make-ups

This year, Rotarians traveled the world in search of make-ups. Canadian make-ups included Ron Oliver in Banff, Canada, and Jim Hughes and Kay North both reported make-ups in Whistler, British Columbia, Canada. Other travelers were Mary Colacicco, Oslo, Norway; G. T. Frost, Cowers, Isle of Wight; Bruce Blakley, Seville, Spain; Lucy Killea, Dublin, Ireland; Bruce Frost, Kuala Lumpur, Malaysia; John Reid, Sydney, Australia; Don Spanninga, Tortola, British Virgin Islands; John Ahlering, Miraj, India; Joe Horiye, Kaohsiung Lighthouse, Taiwan; and Karen Bishop, Puerto Vallarta, Mexico. Those cruising this year included Barbara Anderson, G. T. Frost, Jay Goodwin, Yvonne Larsen, and Patti Roscoe.

Board of Directors, 2001–2002

Paul J. Hartley, Jr., President	John S. Hawkins
Frank V. Arrington, President-elect	Richard W. Jackson
James M. Hughes, Secretary	Patricia L. "Patti" Roscoe
Thomas R. Vecchione, MD, Treasurer	Nancy Scott
Mark C. Trotter, Past President	Richard A. Troncone
Michael W. Brunker	Diana D. Venable
Barbara "Bink" Cook	Geri Warnke
Albert T. Harutunian III	

Former Charger Billy Ray Smith shared memories and discussed prospects for the Chargers and the Aztecs. John Butler, executive vice president and general manager of the San Diego Chargers, shared his stories of turning the team around from last year's 1-15 to this year's 5-11-0.

John Reid, longtime Holiday Bowl leader, reported that the upcoming December 28 game would pit the University of Washington Huskies against a team to be determined after the Big 12 Conference Championship game on December 1. Rick Neuheisel, head football coach of the University of Washington, presented the December 6 program about his team, their latest season, and the excitement he and his players felt about coming to San Diego. "San Diego," he stated, "is the number-one destination of any bowl game in the country." The game between the Texas Longhorns (10-2) and the Washington Huskies (8-3) resulted in a 47-43 win for the Longhorns.

Programs also provided entertainment and a welcome break from a busy day at work. Magician extraordinaire William Gillis III wowed the room with his flying bowling balls and flaming twenty-dollar bills. Juilliard graduate Jacquelyne Silver, a former assistant to Leonard Bernstein, shared behind-the-scenes stories of her years working with Marilyn Horne, Dame Joan Sutherland, and Placido Domingo. Currently, she conducts seminars on managing stage fright (which she did not exhibit).

In another entertaining program, former *Union Tribune* cartoonist Steve Kelly presented a slideshow of odd newspaper articles and signs he collected over the years. *Rotator* Editor of the Week Hal Gardner wanted to hire him, but Steve wanted five dollars per cartoon. A good time was had by all!

San Diego Regional Updates

Memorable programs that featured local institutions, organizations, and personalities brought Rotarians up to date on happenings in San Diego… and beyond.

San Diego Zoo Ambassador Joan Embrey delighted members and guests at the annual Staff Appreciation Day Program on April 25. Her "special guests" included a pair of cheetahs. Although they demonstrated impeccable manners, they looked suspiciously like they would enjoy a good snack.

Des McAnuff emphasized all that the La Jolla Playhouse has contributed to San Diego as well as the theater world in general. He spoke about the many plays that started in La Jolla and ended up on Broadway's Great White Way and London's West End.

◢ Des McAnuff from the La Jolla Playhouse (left) and President Hartley caught up after the meeting.

Several Club 33 members presented news and updates from their industries, including Cecil Steppe, San Diego Urban League; William D. Gore, the FBI special agent in charge; and new member Thella F. Bowens, San Diego International Airport. She told the audience that proposals for a new airport have been narrowed to twenty-one, including Baja, the Imperial Valley, Miramar, Indian land, and a "floating airport" concept. Rotarians eagerly awaited the final decision.

Educators are Both Popular and Informative Speakers

With a strong interest in the local educational scene, Rotarians heard from representatives of UC San Diego (UCSD), San Diego State University (SDSU), the community college district, and the San Diego Unified School District. In addition, programs were presented by leaders from specialized schools and programs that assist young students in under-represented categories.

The first educational program of the year featured Rotarian Stephen Weber, president of SDSU. Weber spoke about the university's economic and social impact on the community: 80,000 alumni in the region, an annual $5-billion budget, and its strong commitment to community service including its partnership with the Price Charities and the remarkable number of volunteer hours contributed by faculty and students.

UCSD Curator Mary Livingston Beebe brought a program in January about a local treasure, the Stuart Collection, an internationally renowned public art collection displayed across the entire UCSD campus. Charles F.

Kennel, director of the Scripps Institution of Oceanography (SIO), presented "Scripps Institution of Oceanography: A San Diego Organization Thinking Globally." He spoke about global warming in the world's oceans, regional climate forecasting, and atmospheric haze, all currently being addressed by SIO.

In addition, there were programs from San Diego Community College District Chancellor Augustine Gallego and Alan Bersin, superintendent of public education, San Diego City Schools. Former California first lady Gayle Wilson dropped by on October 11 and brought news of COSMOS, a California state summer school program designed to enhance interest in math and science.

Former high school English teacher Mary Catherine Swanson, who founded Advancement Via Individual Determination (AVID) in 1980, updated members on the success of the program. Today 65,000 students are enrolled in twenty-one states and fifteen countries, and they go on to college at a 95-percent rate! In September 2001, Swanson was named "America's Best Teacher" by *Time* magazine and CNN.

Barbara Plough, a member of the Ramona Rotary Club, presented "San Pasqual Academy: A Bridge to Knowledge, Support & Hope." Administered by the San Diego County Office of Education, Juvenile Court, and community schools, San Pasqual is the first public residential academy for foster teenagers in the United States. The project houses sixty-two teenagers living in campus homes with foster parents who provide a safe, stable, and caring home environment.

Perhaps best known for the yummiest fish tacos on the planet, Ralph Rubio shared the story of the Cabo Café and Grill, located next to Monarch High School. With Rubio's guidance, the café was named, designed, and is run by students who demonstrate good attendance, good grades, and are living lessons in free enterprise and hard work. Rubio and other community leaders built the restaurant through donations of time, talent, treasure, and materials.

Bio/Medical Powerhouse

San Diego is internationally known for research in various bio/medical subjects, and the region boasts several leaders in the health industry. Throughout the year, Rotarians heard about discoveries, research, and trends in the fields of the human brain, the aging population, the importance of organ donation, affordable healthcare, and health insurance.

Richard Murphy, president and CEO of the Salk Institute, spoke about the role of the prestigious La Jolla institution in basic scientific research in neuroscience and molecular-cellular biology and genetics. Dr. Leon J. Thal, chairman of the Department of Neurosciences at UCSD, presented an update on Alzheimer's

disease. Dr. Stuart Lipton, professor and director of the Del W. Webb Center for Neurosciences and Aging at the Burnham Institute, presented "Emerging Treatments for Degenerative Diseases of the Brain" with particular emphasis on age-related memory loss.

Additional speakers on industry-related topics included Sharie Shipley of LifeSharing on organ donation and John Warner, executive vice president of the Science Applications International Corporation (SAIC), on San Diego's healthcare infrastructure. Also, Dr. Robert K. Ross, former head of Health & Human Services for San Diego County, now president and CEO of The California Endowment, presented a program about the importance of public/private partnerships in attaining health coverage for working families.

Strong Military Presence

For decades, San Diego has been home to military services including the U.S. Navy, the U.S. Marine Corps, the U.S. Air Force, and the U.S. Coast Guard. Each year, Club 33 welcomes citizens who serve in the armed forces. During the year, programs were presented from representatives of the Navy, Marines, Air Force, and Veterans Affairs.

Vice Admiral John Nathman, USN presented "The Need to Recapitalize Aging Ships and Aircraft." General Eugene E. Habiger, USAF (Ret.) spoke about "Terrorism: Changes in Business Since 9/11." Anthony J. Principi, secretary of Veterans Affairs, the federal government's second-largest department, educated Rotarians about the department's vast responsibilities, including the nationwide

▲ President Hartley (left) welcomed Vice Admiral John Nathman (center) and Sheriff Bill Kolender at a meeting.

Economic Forecast

Don Bauder and Bill Holland presented the Economic Forecast for their thirteenth consecutive year. The prediction from Holland was that 2002 should be the best year of the decade! He expected a Dow of 16,000 by the middle of the decade and 30,000 by the end. Bauder expressed more caution and said the recession isn't over. Holland's year-end prediction was 13,000; Bauder's was 11,500. The Dow Jones closed on December 31, 2002, at 8,342.

▲ Rotary International President Rick King (left) was greeted by Rotarians Vince Mudd and Barry Lorge.

system of healthcare services, benefits, programs, and cemeteries for America's veterans and their dependents. Staff Sergeant Michael Arnold, USMC, told of his role in the longest amphibious assault in Marine Corps history. The Marine 15th Expeditionary Unit was the first to enter Pakistan and Afghanistan after 9/11. In a spellbinding interview thoughtfully crafted by Rotarian Clark Anthony, Arnold described "opportunities" provided by the Marines such as hanging on a rope from a helicopter, carrying a 150-pound pack, and living in a shoulder-deep hole for forty-five days. A tumultuous standing ovation closed out the meeting.

THE ROAST

Captain Paul Hartley Walks the Plank

In fitting Navy tradition and hilarious Rotary tradition, Captain Paul Hartley was piped to the chair for the last time on June 27 at 19:30 GMT (half past twelve for those with a civilian clock). Almost-past president Paul was presented with several honorary awards, including the "Smart Dresser Award." Craig Evanco tried to give Paul's sports jacket to Goodwill, but they refused. Past president Paul removed his Rotary president's pin and placed it on new president Frank Arrington's lapel. After an enthusiastic rendition of "Anchors Aweigh," President Frank promptly fined Paul for not wearing his pin—a fitting way to salute Club 33's fine-happy past president!

▲ Craig Evanco channeled his inner Paul Hartley, Jr. by wearing a sports jacket rejected by Goodwill.

▲ Longtime Club 33 member Shelly Brockett serenaded the group.

▲ Executive Director Chet Lathrop congratulated President Hartley on his successful year as president.

▲ President Hartley inspected Mayor Murphy's Rotary lapel pin at the roast.

▲ Mayor Dick Murphy (right) added his congratulations to the Hartleys.

▲ Natasha Josefowitz and Paul Hartley celebrated the presence of women in Club 33 activities.

▲ The past presidents turned out in full force for Hartley's roast.

Salute to Local Heroes, January 17

Since 1991, the Rotary Club of San Diego has sponsored the awards ceremony honoring local heroes. Two heroes each were presented by Sheriff Bill Kolender, District Attorney Paul Pfingst, and Police Chief Dave Bejarano. This year's honorees included Dr. Brad Silva, a South Bay dentist and Navy Reserve commander; Crystal Sanchez; Carmen Miranda; and ten-year-old Gustavo Mendoza. This annual program reminds Rotarians of the many local citizens who assist San Diego law enforcement agencies at the risk of their own safety.

▲ *Attendees at the annual Salute to Local Heroes luncheon included (from left) Sheriff Bill Kolender, Police Chief David Bejarano, Rotarian Bob Arnhym, and District Attorney Paul Pfingst.*

Mr. San Diego: Robert Breitbard, July 26, 2001

Past president and Chair of the Day Bill McDade introduced past Mr./Ms. San Diego award-winners in the audience and shared a little history. The award was started in 1952, but has been presented by past presidents of Rotary Club 33 since 1976. Each year, on the evening of the induction of the new president, the past presidents meet for dinner, review the nominees for Mr./Ms. San Diego, and decide on that year's honoree. Pete Wilson, former San Diego mayor and former governor, introduced the honoree. Perhaps best known for his involvement with the local sports scene as a player, coach, team owner, builder, and benefactor, Bob Breitbard was owner of the San Diego Rockets from 1967 to 1991 and the San Diego Gulls. He established the Breitbard Hall of Fame at Balboa Park in 1953. He was honored for his many contributions to the city, including museums and the Old Globe Theater.

▲ *Pauline des Granges added her congratulations to Bob Breitbard, Mr. San Diego 2001.*

21

Fleet Week, October 8

Admiral Pete Heckman, luncheon chair, noted that this was one of the few "Fleet Week" programs in the nation not cancelled due to 9/11. Special guest speaker was Dale Dye, a consultant to Hollywood studios on war movies, who prepared Tom Hanks for his role in *Saving Private Ryan*. Security was tight at MCAS Miramar, but thanks to advance planning, appropriate photo IDs displayed by all attendees, lots of cooperation, and a shuttle bus arranged by Rotarian John Hawkins, Club 33 members and guests enjoyed the Annual Enlisted Recognition luncheon. Over 600 people attended, and $15,000 was contributed to the Fleet Week Foundation.

Sweethearts Day

▲ *President Hartley serenaded his wife, Charlotte, at the February Sweethearts Day luncheon.*

▲ *Gene Rumsey, Sr. and his wife, Althea, enjoyed the Sweethearts Day luncheon and program.*

MacLaggan Award

Sandra Arkin was honored on December 13 for many good works and the founding of the Children's Museum.

———————————

San Diego Promise Award

The San Diego Promise Award was presented to Club 33 for work on behalf of children and youth at the San Diego Promise organization's website launch by special guest Arnold Schwarzenegger. The award was accepted by Mark Trotter on behalf of the club. Also honored at the event was past president Fred Baranowski for his personal commitment to youth. Sandra McBrayer, CEO of the Children's Initiative, facilitates the San Diego Promise efforts.

———————————

◢ Paul Hartley, Jr.; Scott Kaats, co-owner of Bycor Construction; Susan Armenta, head teacher of Monarch School; and Bink Cook.

CHAPTER TWO

Frank V. Arrington

2002–2003

> *"Experience the good feeling derived from a hands-on club activity!"*

◢ CHANGE OF COMMAND

Due to the Fourth of July holiday, the induction of Frank V. Arrington took place on July 11. A seemingly kinder and gentler Paul Hartley, Jr. introduced the new president and transferred the president's pin from his lapel to that of Arrington. Let the record show that President Arrington's first order of business was to fine past president Hartley who was—at that moment—astonishingly pin-less!

The new president announced his theme for the year: "Club 33: San Diego's Forum for Partnerships in Service." He pledged to continue efforts with San Diego's youth and senior organizations and to expand the community's workforce to provide jobs for challenged applicants. President Arrington encouraged Club 33 members to "experience the good feeling derived from a hands-on club activity." He also announced that he would donate a wheelchair to a project on behalf of each of the speakers for the entire year.

◢ President Frank Arrington made a strong statement at his first meeting as president of Club 33.

SERVICE ABOVE SELF

Wheelchairs for Malawi

As soon as he received his president's gavel, Arrington, along with past president and District Governor Bill McDade, shared details about the second Operation Malawi. District 5340's goal was to raise $50,000 in August to purchase and ship 500 wheelchairs to Malawi. Geri Warnke served as project chair and kept members enthused throughout the year. By the end of July, sixty chairs had been donated. Bill Ward announced that he would purchase twelve wheelchairs to be dedicated to the person making the greatest donation to the Rotary Foundation in the coming year. In October, it was announced that Club 33 had donated over $25,000 for wheelchairs, and the District donations totaled over $165,000. Bill McDade invited Rotarians to join him on his upcoming trip to Malawi to present the chairs. When he returned in December, he reported that orthopedic work had progressed in Blantyre and that he had been present for the opening of the new Children's Hospital. He stated that all the equipment from Operation Malawi was being used and the need for wheelchairs continues. In May, McDade proudly announced that 1,920 chairs had been delivered to Malawi (the goal was 500), $180,000 had been raised (the goal was $50,000), and Club 33 and District 5340 were number one in all of Rotary!

Mercy Outreach Surgical Team (MOST)

Thirteen years ago, three Rotarians, Patricia Robinson, Tom Armstrong, MD, and Tom Vecchione, MD, started the Mercy Outreach Surgical Team (MOST). Components of the

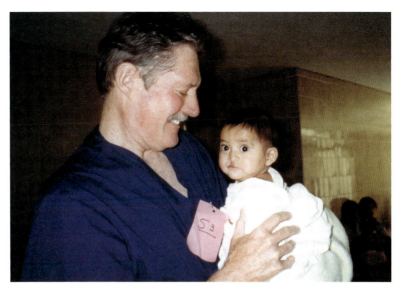

project include Mercy Day in San Diego, surgical visits in Mexico, and follow-up treatment here in San Diego. This year, Mercy Day was held on September 20–23. During a recent trip to Zamora, Mexico, 247 children received surgical treatment. In an October meeting, Vecchione presented an award-winning documentary produced by his filmmaking daughters that captured the feeling and emotion of a MOST visit to Tehuacan in 1999. The twenty-two-member team was in Jalapa, Veracruz, Mexico, from February 21 to March 1, and they completed 254 cases, including 110 crossed eyes and 144 plastic surgeries. Arrington shared that a highlight of his year as president-elect was accompanying the team to Mexico in March 2002. Not only did he spend time with the kids and their families helping to entertain and escort them around, he also actually observed some surgeries.

▲ A highlight of Arrington's year as president-elect was accompanying the MOST team on a trip to Mexico. Here he is shown with a young patient.

Youth Activities

Club 33 continued its longtime enthusiasm and support of various youth-related activities. The Student Recognition Committee was ably chaired by Lisa Miller, MD, and for a month during the school year, Rotary hosted three high school students and their counselor. School Partnership Chair Wayne Goodermote promoted mentoring students at Wilson, Hoover, and Sherman high schools by encouraging Rotarians to spend about an hour a week reading to students.

Youth is an important part of the mission of Rotary. In June, Club 33 received an educational update from Ronne Froman regarding the San Diego City Schools.

In partnership with the Price Foundation, Club 33 helped fund work being done by the Interact Club at Hoover High School. Through the Youth Exchange Program, for the first time in fifteen years, six students were sent on a summer trip of a lifetime. Chuck Pretto served as chair of the Host Committee and during a June meeting, Wayne Goodermote introduced those six students who would spend the summer in Europe. Hosts included Mark Allan, Ellen Casey, Jim Frost, Tom Gehring, Wayne Goodermote, Debi Ives, George Carter Jessop, Yvonne Murchinson, and Patti Roscoe. Pretto, with his wife, Kim, and their family, hosted a BBQ for all the students at his home.

Under the leadership of Tennis Chair Sandy Purdon, the After School Tennis Program Field Day, arranged by Youth Tennis San Diego and the George Barnes Tennis Center, was held on May 10. Over 1,200 young tennis players participated.

Senior Programs

An August program was presented by Pamela Smith, the director of Aging and Independent Services for San Diego County. Her fact-filled program compared the U.S. model of aging in 1902 (average wage: twenty-

two cents; life expectancy: forty-seven years; no retirement system) with the more upbeat model for 2002. The average life span is now seventy-seven years, and many people will spend twenty-six years or more in retirement. She reminded the audience of the need to create both the community and the quality of life we want.

A popular program began in 1999, when B. J. Spitler convened a group to represent seniors in the community. At that time, four seniors were treated to lunch once a month and entertained their tablemates with stories about their careers and experiences. A ninety-two-year-old guest told the harrowing tale of her escape from Panama during World War II. Many senior visitors exemplified the Rotary mission: "Service Above Self." About two years later, the program was expanded to invite one hundred disadvantaged seniors to enjoy the annual Holiday Luncheon in December.

MEMBERSHIP

Fellowship, Camaraderie, and Engagement

During the year, Mayor Dick Murphy reached deep into Club 33's membership for positions on important city boards and commissions, including Nikki Clay to a Citizens Task Force on Chargers Issues, Martha Dennis and Craig Irving to the San Diego Science and Technology Commission, Mike Madigan to the San Diego County Water Authority Board, John Littrell to the Building Appeals and Advisors Board, Tom Day to the Local Enforcement Agency Hearing Panel, and Joe Horiye to the Senior Affairs Advisory Board.

Universities place tremendous value on Rotarians who serve on governing boards. William Geppert was elected to the Board of Trustees of the University of San Diego. Herman Gadon, PhD was elected to the UCSD Board of Overseers. Alice Hayes, president of the University of San Diego, was appointed to the Catholic Church's new twelve-member national review board.

George Olmstead was elected chair of the board of Meals on Wheels, Greater San Diego, Inc. Hal Sadler was named new chairman of the Centre City Development Corporation. Ken Andersen was named board president of the Maritime Museum of San Diego. Karen Hutchens was appointed chair of the San Diego World Trade Center Board of Directors. Gary Meads and Mike Murphy were named to the Board of Directors of the YMCA of San Diego County. Jerry Sanders was named chair of the 2002–2003 United Way/CHAD Campaign Cabinet.

Local and Regional Organizations
Honor Club 33 Members

The San Diego Historical Society honored Dallas Clark and his wife, Mary, and Bob Witty with History Makers 2002 awards. Mary and Dallas received the George W. Marston Award for Distinction in Civic Leadership, and Bob Witty received the San Diego Historical Society Legacy Award. Robert Horsman received the "Nice Guy of the Year" award from The Nice Guys, a local charitable non-profit group. He also received a "Director of the Year" award for ethical conduct, integrity, and corporate leadership from the Corporate Directors Forum. Pauline des Granges and Phil Klauber each received the Balboa Park

Millennium Society's 2001 Millennium Award. Together they have 148 combined years of volunteerism to the park.

Joe Craver received the Golden Achievement Award from the Boys and Girls Clubs of Greater San Diego. Mayor Dick Murphy received the Convisionary Award at the ConVis annual meeting. Elliott Cushman received a James C. Haugh Distinguished Service Award from Sharp Healthcare. Jamie Tucker was named one of the Salvation Army's "Women of Dedication." Martha Dennis received an Athena Pinnacle Award for "Individual in Technology." Bob Fletcher received the Bill Ray Award for his life-long work in recreational fishing and contributions to marine conservatism. Darlene Davies was named "Outstanding Alumna" by the Mortar Board of San Diego County. She also received the SDSU Technology Innovation Award.

In addition, Herb Klein was honored by the San Diego City Council with a resolution proclaiming June 2 as "Herb Klein Day," and "Mary Walshok Day" was proclaimed on May 20 by the San Diego City Council.

Malin Burnham, Herb Klein, and Suzy Spafford were the 2002 Junior Achievement honorees of the San Diego Business Hall of Fame.

Various industries honored Rotarians for their hard work during the year. Jack Berkman and his staff won five Edward J. Nernays Mark of Excellence awards from the Public Relations Society of America, San Diego Chapter. Attorney Sandy Mayberry will serve as co-chair of the 20th Annual Winter Seminar presented by the San Diego Bar Association's Certified Family Law Specialists Committee. The Starcom 2003 Awards, sponsored by Rancho Santa Fe Technology and the *San Diego Business Journal*, presented the Lifetime Achievement Award to Malin Burnham and the "Business Person of the Year" award to William Geppert.

Bill Kolender was named to the Board of Corrections by Governor Gray Davis. David Bejarano was named by President Bush to head the U.S. Marshals Service in San Diego, and he also was honored with a Peacemaker Award by the San Diego Mediation Center.

Health-related organizations honored numerous Rotarians this year. Cheryl and Ron Kendrick were honored by the Huntington's Disease Society of America. Katherine Kennedy and Douglas Wilson were named to the board of the Sidney Kimmel Cancer Center. Jerry Sanders was elected chairman of the board of the San Diego/Imperial Counties Chapter of the Red Cross, and six Rotarians were named to the board of the local Red Cross Chapter, including Phil Blair, Joe Craver, William Geppert, Ben Haddad, Richard Ledford, and Jerry Sanders.

Cultural venues benefited from the support of Club 33 members. Jim Fitzpatrick and his wife, Jan, chaired the opening of the theater in the Performing Arts Center at the Salvation Army Ray and Joan Kroc Community Center. Joyce Glazer was selected to chair the Mingei International Museum's twenty-fifth anniversary celebration. George Gilred served as co-chair of the 2003 Lindbergh Awards event at the San Diego Aerospace Museum. Geri Warnke was co-chair of the La Jolla Playhouse expansion drive, and Phil Blair co-chaired the fourth annual BRAVO! staged by the Performing Arts League at the Westgate Hotel. Ronne Froman was named the event chair for Fleet Week 2003 in San Diego.

In January, Diana Venable received the Rotary International Four Avenues of Service Award.

Significant birthdays were celebrated by Lou Wax, who celebrated his ninetieth on December 30, and Ferd Fletcher, who celebrated his ninety-second on June 5.

In June, Gary London rode into a meeting on the first Segway the club had ever seen.

Time for Fun

Rotarians availed themselves of a variety of social events that promoted fellowship, engagement, and tons of fun. The annual Day at the Races kicked off the social season in August. September brought a "Swinging for Seniors" golf tournament at Steel Canyon Golf Course benefiting Market Square Manor, a low-income complex for seniors, and the annual Rotary Sail and BBQ was held at the San Diego Yacht Club. A Club 33 RV fellowship took place in October at the Royal Pines RV Park, Idyllwood. Spring found members enjoying a Rotary fishing trip. Bonnie Schwartz made history in June at the Club 33 golf tournament at the La Jolla Country Club. Not only was she the first woman to play at the club, she was the first woman overall champ. Yeah, Bonnie!

PROGRAMS

A major component of Rotary life is being informed and involved in and around the region and this year was no exception as Rotarians learned about exciting and interesting things taking place in business and industry, military affairs, medical research, education, and sports and entertainment.

Business

Peter Hall, president of Center City Development Corporation, led off the year. William D. Jones, president and CEO of CityLink Investment Corporation and noted developer of the award-winning eight-block City Heights Urban Village, brought an update. Rotarians also heard from Maureen Stapleton, general manager, San Diego County Water Authority; Laurence G. Fitch, president/CEO, San Diego Workforce Partnership, Inc.; George Chamberlain, business editor, KOGO "Economic Straight Talk"; Bonnie Dumanis, district attorney; Alex Montoya, senior membership coordinator, San Diego County Hispanic Chamber of Commerce; and Gail Goldberg, planning director, City of San Diego, who noted that San Diego expects to

▲ Doug O'Brien, Joyce Glazer, and Frank and Linnea Arrington visited at a special event.

add one million residents by 2030, bringing 650,000 additional cars to the region.

Cathy Anderson, CEO of the San Diego Film Commission, talked about TV shows *Silk Stalkings* and *Hunter*, starring SDSU alum Fred Dryer, and movies *Top Gun* and *Traffic*,

Foreign/Exotic Make-ups

This was a big year for travel and more Rotarians ventured to faraway places. Reporting make-ups were Larry Clapper, Aarhus West Rotary Club, Denmark; Barbara Bry, Dublin, Ireland; Dick Jackson, St. Martin Nord Club, Virgin Islands; Margaret Larkin, Moscow and St. Petersburg, Russia; Tracy Lau, Paris, France; Joan Friedenberg, Whistler Millennium Club, British Columbia, Canada; Judy McDonald, Edinburgh, Scotland; Al Haruntunian, Toronto, Canada; Ian Campbell, London, England; Don Spanninga, New South Wales, Australia; Pat Rogondino, Frankfurt, Germany; Bill McColl, St. John, U.S. Virgin Islands; Sam Carpenter, Granada, Spain; George Olmstead, Freeport, Grand Bahamas; Jim Hughes, Brisbane and Sidney Cove, Australia; and Bill McDade, Hokitika, New Zealand. Travelers heading south included Ed Kitrosser, Ixtapa, Mexico; Chip Goodwin and Bob Fletcher, both to the San Felipe North Club, Mexico; and Bill Ward, Sam Carpenter, Doug Arbon, Tom Vecchione, Bob Cairncross, and Joe Davies to Jalapa, Mexico. Frank Arrington, Bink Cook, Karen Green, Joe DeCristofaro, and Jim Hughes reported make-ups in Barcelona while attending the Rotary International Convention. Bill McDade made up meetings in Limbe, Lilongwe, Blantyre, and Mzuzu in Malawi, Africa.

Rotarians enjoyed life on the high seas, and still found time for make-ups! Cruisers included Will Newbern, *Nordic Express*; Bob Witty, *QE2*, near Cape Town, South Africa; Chuck Duddles, *Norwegian Dream*; Don Spanniga, *Norwegian Dream*; Bill McDade, *Prinsendam*; Ross Pyle, *Prinsendam*; Karen Green, *Rhapsody of the Seas*; Margaret Larkin, *Celebrity*; and Warner Harrah, *Ryndam*. Will Newbern also made up two meetings around Cape Horn.

New Members

NAME	PRIMARY SPONSOR
Craig Andrews, Brobeck, Phleger & Harrison, LLP	Jim Goode
Ruben Andrews, Graphic Solutions	Ray Robbins
Ray Ashley, Maritime Museum Association of San Diego	Ken Andersen
Bruce Binkowski, Pacific Life Holiday Bowl	John Reid
Edward D. Brady, Booz Allen Hamilton	Sarah Lamade
Mary Brigden, Oracle	Sarah Lamade
Dennis Burks, SeaWorld San Diego	George Gildred
Tony Calabrese, Combined Health Agencies	Jamie Tucker
Cathryn Campbell, Campbell & Flores	Barbara Bry
Hal Clement, KGTV	Robert Horsman
Doris Davies, SCME Mortgage Banking	Joe Davies
Ignacio De La Torre, SBC-Pacific Bell	Joanne Pastula
Archdeacon William F. Dopp, The Episcopal Diocese of San Diego	Paul J. Hartley, Jr.
Rodger W. Dougherty, Kaiser Permanente	Dennis Humberstone
John Driscoll, Driscoll Yachts	Paul J. Hartley, Jr.
William K. Geppert, Cox Communications	Dick Troncone
Robert Gillingham, Francis Parker School	Ed Glazener
Richard Gulley, Alliant Insurance Services	George Driver
David Gundstrom, Marvin K. Brown	Debbie Day
Michael Hager, Museum of Natural History	Pat Crowell
Katherine Harrington, The T Sector	Martha Dennis
Paul J. Hartley III, Prudential California Realty	Charlie Brauel
David T. Hayhurst, PhD, SDSU	Steve Weber
Charles L. Hellerich, Luce, Forward, Hamilton & Scripps	Bill McKenzie
Betty M. Hubbard, Community Volunteer	Paul J. Hartley, Jr.
Howard Justus, Debit Acquisition Company of America	Marten Barry
James R. Kitchen, PhD, SDSU	Steve Weber
Brian P. Lange, Perim Consulting	Roy Lange
R. Merl Ledford, Scripps Clinic (Ret.)	Richard Ledford
Cinda K. Lucas, In Sync	Peg Eddy
James Moss, JEM Trust (Ret.)	Debbie Day
Clifford O. Myers III, Marine Corps Recruit Depot	Ronne Froman
Gail K. Naughton, SDSU	Steve Weber
Doug O'Brien, The Salvation Army	Joyce Glazer
Alfred Panico, Waitt Family Foundation	Judy McDonald
Andrew L. Poat, City of San Diego	Michael Uberuaga
Stephen Porter, Customs Brokers	Homer D. Peabody, Jr., MD

(continued on next page)

(continued from previous page)

NAME	PRIMARY SPONSOR
Joe Sczempa, San Diego Employees Association	unknown
Kathleen Sridhar, Indus Technology, Inc.	unknown
Raymond Uzeta, Chicano Federation of San Diego County	Richard Ledford
Charles Van Vechten, Van Vechten Creative Communications	Mark Allan
Barbara Warden, Downtown San Diego Partnership	Nikki Clay

In Memoriam

John M. Berry	John Howard Norton (Honorary Member)
Donald E. Clark	Leland D. Pratt
William J. Cox, MD	Will D. Rudd
Robert E. Harris	Thomas A. Shumaker
Dan O. Henry	Aubrey Thompson
Rear Admiral Joe Howard, USN (Ret.)	Jamie Tucker
Robert A. Leonard	George Westphal

Rotarians of the Quarter

Harney Cordua	Scott McClendon
Bob Russell	Tom Mosher
Suzy Spafford	Paul Woo
Bonnie Schwartz	

▲ *President Frank Arrington presented Bob Russell with a Rotarian of the Quarter certificate.*

Grotarian Events

In addition to learning Rotary history and traditions, Grotarians had fun getting to know one another at the Scripps Institution of Oceanography pier and at the San Diego ballpark. A third event was a scenic tour of San Diego on an amphibious vehicle.

▲ *President Arrington enjoyed a kayak ride at the Grotarian outing at SeaWorld.*

▲ *President Arrington and Ellen Casey enjoyed watching the antics of the SeaWorld polar bears at a Grotarian event.*

Board of Directors, 2002–2003

Frank V. Arrington, President

Patricia L. "Patti" Roscoe, President-elect

Thomas R. Vecchione, MD, Secretary

James M. Hughes, Treasurer

Paul J. Hartley, Jr., Past President

Michael W. Brunker

Barbara "Bink" Cook

Daryl E. "Debbie" Day

Stanford F. Hartman, Jr.

Albert T. Harutunian III

John S. Hawkins

Richard W. Jackson

Barry S. Lorge

Richard A. Troncone

Geri Warnke

all filmed in San Diego. Daniel P. Brannigan, senior director of community affairs for Pfizer, Inc., the largest pharmaceutical company in the United States, reported that Pfizer recently opened an 800,000-square-foot research campus in La Jolla. Irwin Jacobs, chairman and CEO of Qualcomm, demonstrated a tiny little phone that someday would be a part of everyone's lives. He shared the latest information on their work on Code Division Multiple Access (CDMA) and their ongoing success as the world's fastest-growing wireless communications technology company.

Medical Research and Health

In addition to a robust business and commercial life, San Diego is surrounded by world-class health and research organizations. This year, programs included speakers Albert Deisseroth, MD of Kimmel Cancer Center and Dani S. Grady, director of Development & Institute Relations for the San Diego Cancer Research Institute. A panel including City Council member Jim Madaffer, Fire Chief Jeff Bowman, and community leader Karen McElliott presented "Saving Lives with AED: San Diego Project Heart Beat."

Sports

San Diegans (and Rotarians) are noted for their love of sports. Teams from Friday Night Lights to the pros are enthusiastically cheered on. Programs included Head Basketball Coach Steve Fisher of SDSU; Bruce Binkowski, executive director of the Holiday Bowl, who presented a video of great Holiday Bowl games; and Coach Jim Walden, whose Washington State team played Brigham Young University in 1981. Asked to predict the point spread of the upcoming Holiday Bowl game between Kansas and Arizona, he wisely answered, "One team will score more than the other!"

In addition, Club 33 members learned about the growth of the Super Bowl and received updates from local pro teams, including updates from Padres Vice President and Senior Advisor Dave Winfield and Chargers Head Coach Marty Schottenheimer.

Chandler Tagliabue, representing Kick-off to Rebuild, and Patricia Johnson, representing Rebuilding Together, presented information regarding their partnership with the NFL in 252 cities (including San Diego) and the rehabilitation work accomplished in over 8,000 homes. They will sponsor the rebuilding of two homes in San Diego during Super Bowl Week.

Higher Education

Walk around the campuses of our extraordinary institutions of higher learning and just feel your IQ grow! San Diegans are lucky to have a plethora of higher education opportunities. A panel titled "San Diego in the Knowledge Age" included speakers Chancellor Robert Dynes, UCSD; President Alice Hayes, USD; and President Stephen Weber, SDSU. Other academic presenters during the year included Dean Gail G. Naughton, SDSU, College of Business, and Dean Thomas J. Campbell, UC Berkeley, Haas School of Business.

Military

Although known to many as a "Navy town," San Diego is also home to the other services, and Rotarians enjoy a long history with and strong connection between the military and the business community. The Military Affairs Committee encouraged Club 33 Rotarians to support service men and women and their families and, to no one's surprise, members went above and beyond the call of duty! Club 33 contributed $5,250 to the Navy Wives Food Locker, established in memory of John Berry, a San Diego "institution" and unofficial liaison with the U.S. Navy. A Rotarian since 1977, he died in January 2003. Peg Eddy and her husband "adopted" a military family and them helped by picking up kids from school, dropping off meals, and calling to see how they were doing. Dave Gundstrom of

Marvin K. Brown provided car services to families of deployed service men and women through Operation Homefront. Military speakers this year included Rear Admiral Jose Betancourt, U.S. Navy and Major General Jan Huly, U.S. Marine Corps. The annual luncheon honoring

Islam and the West; Dr. Michael J. Sise of Scripps Mercy Trauma Services brought important information regarding preparing for terrorist bombings; and Tony Perry of the *Union Tribune* talked about being embedded with the Marines during the Iraq War.

▲ Special guest
Art Linkletter.

enlisted military was held on October 10, when Club 33 hosted 250 enlisted military men and women.

Beyond San Diego

National and international program topics are always a popular draw. Rotarians welcomed Herbert Klein, who shared stories from "Inside the White House." Astronaut Marsha S. Ivins received an enthusiastic response for her presentation of "Living and Working in Space" and William Simon, Jr. spoke about his candidacy for governor. In addition, Thomas Dillon spoke about homeland security; Robert Kittle of the *Union Tribune* spoke about

Celebrity Guests

It's always fun to meet a few celebrities, and this year, Club 33 enjoyed two delightful celebrity guests, Art Linkletter and Peter Yarrow.

SDSU President Stephen Weber introduced Linkletter and shared that he was a graduate of SDSU, a star basketball player, and a member of the SDSU Basketball Hall of Fame. In addition, he served as student body president. Linkletter's twenty-seventh book is underway, written to help "baby boomers" prepare for their golden years. Introduced by Burt Nestor, Peter Yarrow of Peter Paul and Mary fame grabbed his guitar and led the audience in a sing-along of "Puff, the Magic Dragon," stating that "group singing helps bring us closer together." He explained that each day, up to 150,000 students stay home from school

▲ Peter Yarrow (of Peter, Paul and Mary) and Frank Arrington.

◢ Burt Nestor, Peter Yarrow, and Frank Arrington.

◢ Peter Yarrow entertained the audience.

out of fear of some kind of emotional or physical abuse, which was why he established Operation Respect, the "Don't Laugh at Me" project.

THE ROAST

The Secret Life of Frank Arrington

Wheeled into the room wearing convict stripes, Frank Arrington was about to be roasted. The invocation by Pat Crowell was interrupted by his own cell phone. During a long conversation with Frank's mother, Pat asked if it was possible for Frank to be unintentionally dull, decided that it wasn't, and promptly smashed the cell phone with a hammer. Ross Pyle sang the news of the day which identified Frank as "King of the Dull" and complained of unfair fines. Dick Troncone related Frank's Army experience and told of the offer of a promotion to Private First Class, which Frank declined because he didn't want the responsibility! In his eloquent re-cap of the year, Mark Trotter commented that he was chosen because he had presided over lots of funerals and was used to saying nice things about rascals. On a more serious note, during Frank's year, the number of members who donated to the Paul Harris Fund and $150 to the Club 33 Fund increased from 130 to 330. Frank was noted for upping the fines from one hundred dollars to "a whopping $250!" Total giving as a club was $180,000, and the $25,000 donated for wheelchairs was the highest donation for any Rotary club in the world. In addition to being a star money-getter, Frank gave a wheelchair in honor of each and every speaker. What a year, President Frank!

Camp Enterprise, April 3

Continuing the tradition started in 1976 by Club 33 past president Bruce Moore and former executive director Chet Lathrop, the Camp Enterprise kick-off meeting was held at the U. S. Grant Hotel on April 3. Chaired by Cindy Olmstead, speakers for Camp Enterprise were Elijah Blue Morgan from the School of Performing Arts and B. J. MacPherson, television color analyst for Gulls games broadcast on Cox/Time Warner Channel 4.

Fleet Week, September 26

Chaired by Cindy Olmstead, the meeting was hosted by the Marine Corps Recruit Depot (MCRD). The world-famous MCRD Band entertained with patriotic and jazz music and a piccolo solo of "Stars and Stripes Forever." Major General Jan Huly, MCRD commander, spoke about the history of the Marines in San Diego, which began in the early 1920s. Currently, over 54 percent of all Marines train in San Diego. Over 250 enlisted military men and women attended.

▲ *Military guests showed off their official Fleet Week T-shirts.*

▲ *Roy Lange with a military guest.*

▲ *President Arrington with a military guest.*

▲ *Club 33 members welcomed many members of the local armed forces at the annual Fleet Week luncheon.*

Economic Forecast, January 2

Perennial favorites Don Bauder and Bill Holland presided over the annual Economic Forecast luncheon. Bauder predicted that the Dow Jones Industrial Average would close at 11,500 and Holland predicted 13,000. The Dow closed on December 31, 2003, at 10,454.

Salute to Local Heroes, January 16

The Sheriff's Department honored Colleen Conelly, Santiago Mendoza, and Juan Gauchuz. The San Diego Police Department honored Ron Sulin. The San Diego District Attorney's Office honored Josh Thorburn and the members of the search team that found Danielle Van Damme's body. A Group Organization Award was presented to Bill Guttentag and Kate Adler (standing in for producer Dick Wolfe) for the TV series *Crime and Punishment*, which was filmed in the DA's office.

Paul Harris Dinner, November 16

Co-chaired by Cathy LeClair and Rick Clark of the La Jolla Golden Triangle Club, "An Evening in History" was held at the Museum of Natural History. Committee members included Jack Anthony, Cathy Anderson, Jack Berkman, Ann Bethel, Jo Briggs, Sam Carpenter, Bink Cook, Joe daRosa, Darlene Davies, Janie Davis, Debbie Day, Brad Delaney, Chuck Duddles, Diane Gilabert, Bill Gore, John Hawkins, Jim Hughes, Claudia Johnson, Tracy Lau, Nancy Laturno, Bill McDade, Kay North, Rick Richards, Norm Roberts, Patti Roscoe, Lorin Stewart, Karen Stone, Dick Sullivan, and Diana Venable. The "surprise guest" was none other than Paul Harris! Well, not the real Paul Harris, of course, but District Governor James Young, who was famous for his impersonations of Paul Harris at Rotary events.

Mrs. San Diego: Deborah Szekely, September 5

Deborah Szekely, owner of the Rancho La Puerta health spa in Tecate and The Golden Door in Escondido, joined just three other women who have received the prestigious Rotary award since its inception in 1952. Former governor Pete Wilson presented the award and described Szekely's remarkable career and commitment in both the public and non-profit sectors. Szekely gave a moving account of her emigration from Romania with her husband prior to World War II. More recently, she has concentrated on mentoring future leaders through her Eureka Communities program, and she has founded a museum to honor post-World War II immigrants.

The MacLaggan Award, December 12

Dr. Fred Frye presented Blair Sadler with the MacLaggan Award for his service and commitment to youth. The award was established by an anonymous donor in December 1991 in memory of the late Dr. James MacLaggan, a longtime member of Club 33. The award honors an individual for outstanding contributions to the well-being of children. Dr. Frye was the first honoree in 1991.

In December, District 5340 received a District Service Award from the Rotary International Foundation for participation in the annual program's fund-giving. San Diego Rotary Club was recognized as the number-one club in the district in total giving. Norbert Sanders and President Frank Arrington were cited for outstanding efforts.

▲ From left: Past district governor Ron Beaubien, RI President Rick King (2001–2002), Pauline des Granges, Frank Arrington, and Vince Mudd.

▲ Special guest Santa Claus (a.k.a. Roy Lange) greeted Rotarians Diana Venable (left) and Nancy Scott at the annual Holiday Luncheon.

▲ Linnea and Frank Arrington with Dick Troncone and Peter Duncan.

▲ Craig Evanco, State Senator Christine Kehoe and her guest, Dean Crowder, and Frank Arrington.

CHAPTER THREE

Patricia L. Roscoe

2003–2004

"From day one, I was a Rotarian, and proud to be part of this dynamic, philanthropic, service-oriented organization; I wouldn't trade this year for anything!"

◢ CHANGE OF COMMAND

In 1988, Patricia L. "Patti" Roscoe was the seventh woman to be invited to join Rotary—recruited, in fact, by male members of Club 33. Patti "The Rascal" Roscoe was inducted as president on July 3—her birthday!—and she received the president's gavel and the diamond president's pin. The Marine Corps Recruit Depot Brass Quintet entertained with jazz and patriotic songs and everyone sang "Happy Birthday!" to Roscoe. As her first presidential duty, President Roscoe fined Ian Campbell $2,000—one hundred dollars for each year of his twenty years with the San Diego Opera, setting a new high standard for fines!

The first speaker of the year was Marine Corps Major General Jan Huly, who reviewed his term of duty and his nomination for three stars. Lucky he didn't get fined for that!

SERVICE ABOVE SELF

The summer and fall of 2003 found Club 33-ers involved in many youth-oriented projects. In August, Dick Jackson and his construction team built two new classrooms at the Nicolas Bravo Elementary School in Tijuana. With the Ensenada Centenarian Rotary Club, the Fish Across the Border project continued to lure members' participation. Their efforts resulted in lots of fish as well as money to provide sacks of groceries for needy families in that area. Jay Arnett won the Gene Rumsey Perpetual Trophy with a forty-four-pound albacore.

In October, the MOST team made their trip to Cuernavaca, Mexico, where Dr. Tom Vecchione and his team performed 255 surgeries. In March, they returned and performed 350 additional surgeries. The annual auction in December raised over $25,000 with proceeds going to Outbound Youth Exchange, Senior Services, and the Aseltine School. Homer Peabody, a major supporter of the Youth Tennis San Diego Foundation, reported that, thanks to Rotarians' generosity, over 7,000 young people participate each year.

Ongoing support of seniors continued as Rotarians welcomed visiting seniors each month who added depth and the wisdom of experience to table discussions. The winter bedding and clothing drive for seniors also continued to heat up.

In December, Ray McKewon's company donated a stunning $250,000 for a brush rig for the San Diego Fire Department after the devastating late October Cedar Fire. What a gift!

Last year Bill Ward challenged the membership to support the Rotary Foundation. Ten people stepped up and they were awarded certificates in their honor from the Wheelchair Foundation.

MEMBERSHIP

Fellowship, Camaraderie, and Engagement

A strategic planning process, chaired by Cindy Olmstead and Tom Gehring, began in October when a survey was sent to all members asking for feedback regarding aspects of service, programs, impact on the region, pride in Club 33, reasons for belonging to Rotary, and vision for the future of Club 33. Results and highlights were:

▲ Ray McKewon announced his company's stunning $250,000 gift to the San Diego Fire Department after the October Cedar Fire.

▲ Patti's Posse included (from left): Debbie Day, Patti Roscoe, Nikki Clay, Joyce Gattas, Katherine Kennedy, and Bonnie Schwartz.

▲ Chuck Pretto, a Rotary Youth exchange student, and President Patti Roscoe visited at a meeting.

Camp Enterprise, April 15

Kicking off the popular weekend was speaker Jerry Swain, former sales manager for IBM, successful entrepreneur, and owner of Jer's Handmade Chocolates. He celebrated his third year making chocolate-covered peanut butter balls appropriately named "Chocolate Balls." His mission: to have fun and be profitable. No one argued with that concept!

▲ *Camp Enterprise guest speaker Jerry Swain.*

▲ Club 33's role in San Diego: Leadership

▲ Ways Club 33 can increase its impact on San Diego: Take on one to three major social issues and be very visible

▲ What Club 33 does well: Community service/projects and meetings

▲ What Club 33 can do to improve: Greater member involvement and a broader membership base

▲ Looking ahead to 2008: Enhance service we are doing and enhance member involvement

▲ Reasons to be proud of Club 33: Our people—patriotic, respectful, reverent, and intelligent; Club achievements—Monarch, Camp Enterprise, interaction, mentorships, etc.

On March 11, the vision was announced: "Club 33 will become a diverse team of San Diego's preeminent leaders focused on significant community and international service projects."

At the May 20 meeting, Roscoe announced a "provocative idea" generated through the strategic planning process: the purchase of a permanent Club 33 location for administration, committee meetings, and luncheons. A task force was assigned and will report back to the membership. The search is still in progress.

In June 2004, President-elect Tom Vecchione attended the Rotary International meeting in Osaka, Japan. Once back home, he described the Japanese hosts who shared their heritage in the shrines and architecture of Osaka, Kyoto, and Tokyo. Vecchione pronounced the experience "spectacular in every way."

Members in the News

San Diego Magazine's popular list of "50 People to Watch in 2004" included Rotarians Phil Blair, Thella Bowens, Pete Davis, Ronne Froman, and Mayor Dick Murphy.

Patti Roscoe, Cecil Steppe, and Carol Wallace were named to the panel to select the new police chief for San Diego.

Mayor Dick Murphy reached into Club 33's membership to take advantage of members' experience and talents. His appointments included Tyler Cramer to the San Diego Housing Commission and Gail Naughton to the Science and Technology Commission. Martha Dennis was reappointed to the Science and Technology Commission. Peter Davis was elected chairman of the Port Commission, and he also announced his candidacy for the office of Mayor of San Diego. Wayne Raffesberger and Hal Sadler were reappointed to the Centre City Development Corporation Board of Directors.

Members of Club 33 were pressed into service by other organizations and industry groups. Bob Arnhym was selected chairman of the Board of Trustees of the National Association of Miss America State Pageants. Paul Downey was elected president of the Southern California Elderly Nutrition Partnership. Joyce Glazer was appointed to the National Advisory Board of the Salvation Army. John Hawkins was named 2004 board chairman of the San Diego Regional Chamber of Commerce. Ronne Froman was named interim chair of the Military Affairs Council by the San Diego Regional Chamber of Commerce, and she was nominated as a director of the 1st Pacific Bank of California. She and Greg Zinser joined the Monarch School Board.

Rotarians Recognized by Others for Service Above Self

In the Awards and Honors category, Malin Burnham, chairman emeritus of the USD Real Estate Institute's Policy Advisory Board, received the Daniel F. Mulvihill Leadership Award from the institute. Robert Horsman was honored by the San Diego Chapter of the Association of Fundraising Executives as "Outstanding Development Volunteer." Joe Craver received a Golden Achievement Award from the Boys and Girls Clubs of Greater San Diego and KSWB Cares for Kids. Reint Reinders was named 2003 Spirit of Life Award honoree by the newly

formed San Diego Hospitality and Tourism Industry for City of Hope.

Other organizations bestowing honors included United Way of San Diego, awarding Maureen Stapleton the Volunteer of the Year/Naish Award, and the Lions Club of San Diego, honoring Betty Mohlenbrock with the annual Willis H. L. Fletcher Community Service Award.

Gloria Penner received the 2003 Public Service Award from the San Diego Radio Broadcasters Association, and she was named the first recipient of the League of Women Voters Gloria Penner Award. Dallas Clark and his wife, Mary, were recognized for their combined 112 years of service to Balboa Park at the third annual awards ceremony of the Balboa Park Millennium Society. Phil Blair and Mel Katz were among the 2003 Junior Achievement honorees of the San Diego Business Hall of Fame.

In addition, William Geppert received an honorary award for his many community activities at a civic tribute sponsored by the Copley Family YMCA and KSWB Cares for Kids. Paul Hartley, Jr. and Lou Metzger were among the honorees of the thirteenth annual Essence of Life Awards presented by Elderhelp of San Diego. Michelle Candland received a Director of the Year Award from the Corporate Directors Forum for her work at Monarch School. Bill McColl and his wife, Barbara, received the 2003 Community Champions of the Year Award presented by the San Diego Hall of Champions. Berit Durler was honored as one of the 2003–2004 Volunteers of the Year at the Combined Health Agencies annual event.

Rotarian and Mayor Dick Murphy received two awards: the first Theodore Roosevelt Award for Executive Leadership given by Republicans for Environmental Education, and The Distinguished Alonzo Award, presented at the Downtown San Diego Partnership's Alonzo Awards event. The honor is named after the founder of San Diego, Alonzo Horton. Dick Troncone received a 2004 Monty Award from the SDSU Alumni Association. Ronne Froman and Mike Sise and his wife, Beth, were honored as "Peacemakers" by the San Diego Mediation Center. Bonnie Dumanis received the 2004 Service by a Public District Attorney Award at the San Diego County Bar Association's 2004 service awards event. Maureen Stapleton was named "Headliner of the Year" by the San Diego Press Club. Gerry Wilson received the Paula E. Sullivan Award for Outstanding Career Achievement from the San Diego Advertising Club. Honorary member Doris Howell was inducted into the San Diego County Women's Hall of Fame. Bob Fletcher was inducted into the California Outdoors Hall of Fame at the International Exposition in San Mateo, California. Peg Eddy was recognized as the 2003 "Woman Business Owner of the Year" by the National Association of Women Business Owners. Dr. Herman Gadon was honored by UCSD on the twentieth anniversary of the Executive Program for Scientists and Engineers. He was a founder and the program's first director.

Rotarians Chair Many Fundraisers

Generous with both time and talent, Club 33 members were tapped to lead the planning and execution of many successful fundraisers in the San Diego area. Art Rivkin and his wife, Jeannie, were honorary chairs of a reception/auction to benefit the A. B. and Jessie Polinsky Children's Center. Katherine Kennedy served as chair of the Old Globe fundraising auction.

Cheryl and Ron Kendrick chaired the City of Hope's "Celebration of Hope" to benefit the fight against Huntington's Disease. Phil Blair served as co-chair of the 2003 BRAVO! fundraiser. Patti Roscoe was honorary chair of the YWCA's In the Company of Women Luncheon and also served as co-chair for the dinner celebrating Herb Klein's retirement and his many achievements.

On September 11, Shelly Brockett celebrated his ninetieth birthday!

Fun and Fellowship

The annual Day at the Races provided big fun and small winnings. President Patti Roscoe and Chet Lathrop crowned the winner of the San Diego Rotary Club race. Apparently they picked up some tips as both won modestly in the next race.

September found Rotarians and their guests at the annual Sail and BBQ. That same month, Bonnie Schwartz received the trophy for Best Net Golfer. At the November 1 district dinner at the Town & Country Hotel, Hal Clement surprised Chet Lathrop with a city proclamation declaring November 1 to be "Rotary Foundation of Rotary International Day in San Diego," in recognition of the impact the RI Rotary Foundation has had on the world and the contribution that Club 33's own Chet Lathrop has made to promote the Rotary Foundation. In addition, many Rotarians and guests enjoyed a May winemaker event.

Grotarian Events

Seven Grotarian events occurred, each one more fabulous and interesting than the last. First up was an evening at the Starlight Theater for dinner and a performance of *The Scarlet Pimpernel*. An event at SPAWARS was a big draw. Visits to a few of the "jewels" of San Diego included the San Diego Zoo, the San Diego Museum of Art, and a tour of the USS *Midway*. In addition, Grotarians enjoyed an evening sail aboard the 1914 vessel *Pilot* and a tour of the HMS *Surprise*, which will be featured in the next Russell Crowe film (sadly, he didn't attend), and a "Sail on Big Clipper" completed the events for the year.

Rotarians of the Quarter

Dick Sullivan

Michelle Candland

Cindy Olmstead

Jerry Van Ert

Foreign/Exotic Make-ups

Traveling Rotarians have the opportunity to visit many foreign locations in their quest for make-ups! This year found Rotarians all over the United States, as far west as Hawaii, as far north as Alaska, as far east as Massachusetts, and as far south as, well, San Diego. Out-of-country travelers included Jim Moss, Stockholm, Sweden; John Wertz, Munich, Germany; Paul Hartley, Jr., Budapest, Hungary; Vaughn Lyons, Melbourne and Sydney, Australia; Margaret Larkin, Victoria, British Columbia, Canada; Don Spanninga, Barcelona, Spain; George Carter Jessop, Florence, Italy; Ed Kitrosser, Christchurch and Aukland, New Zealand; Jim Jackson, Kyoto, Japan; Natasha Josefowitz, Herman Gadon, and Bruce Moore, Amsterdam, Belgium; Sandra Schrift, Queenstown and Sydney, Australia; Jerry Doran, Paris, France; Marten Barry, Cabo San Lucas, Mexico; Bill McColl, St. Thomas, Virgin Islands; Joan Friedenberg, Blenheim, New Zealand; and James M. Hughes, Matsue, Japan.

Many Rotarians attended meetings aboard cruise ships, including Newt Pollock, *Sun Princess* and *Statendam*; John Littrell, *Golden Princess*; Berit Durler, *Rotterdam*; Margaret Larkin, *QE II*; Dick Sturgeon, *Celebrity*; Dan Spanninga, *Noordam*; Darlene Davies, *Ryndam*; Geri Warnke, *Legend of the Seas*; Roy Lange, *Ryndam*; Kenny Jones, *Island Princess*; and Karen Green, *Radiance of the Seas*. Bill Herrin enjoyed the maiden voyage of *The World* and Kevin Enright reported his trip on "another 'dam ship."

In Memoriam

Elliott L. Cushman

Arthur J. Jacobs

Margaret Larkin

David E. Porter

B. J. Curry Spitler, PhD

Kathy Sridhar

William K. Tisdale, MD

Dwight E. Twist

Ernest E. Yahnke

Board of Directors, 2003–2004

Patricia L. "Patti" Roscoe, President

Thomas R. Vecchione, MD, President-elect

Daryl E. "Debbie" Day, Secretary

Robert G. Russell, Jr., Treasurer

Frank V. Arrington, Past President

Michael W. Brunker

Richard W. Jackson

Stanford F. Hartman, Jr.

Barry S. Lorge

Lisa S. Miller, MD

Nancy Scott

Suzanne "Suzy" Spafford

Richard A. Troncone

Diana D. Venable

Geri Warnke

New Members

NAME	PRIMARY SPONSOR
Susan Basinger, Higgs, Fletcher & Mack	John Morrell
Patrick W. Caughey, Wimmer, Yamada and Caughey	Robert Noble
Chris Christopher, Jr., Exodus Business Solutions	Larry Clapper
Richard D. Coutts, MD, Orthopaedic Surgery Group of San Diego	Ellen Casey
Jeremiah Doran, Doran Insurance Services	Jim M. Hughes
Marlee Ehrenfeld, MJE Marketing Services, LLC	Phil Blair
Greg Garner, San Diego Credit Association	Paul Hering
William R. Hamlin, Ayres Land Company	Dick Troncone
Isabella Heule, San Diego World Trade Center	Richard Ledford
Jo Dee C. Jacob, Girl Scouts, San Diego-Imperial Council	Joan Friedenberg
Captain Michael Keefe, USN, Naval Medical Center	Darrell Hunsaker
Steve LaDow, LaDow Company	Mike Morton
William S. Littlejohn, Sharp Healthcare Foundation	David Mitchell
Leane Marchese, Elderhelp of San Diego	B. J. Spitler
Timothy McIntyre, Francis Parker School	Chuck Pretto
Curtis Nelson, Silicon Space, Inc.	unknown
Paul Nestor, Paul Nestor Photography	Burt Nestor
Paul Palmer, Big Brothers & Sisters of San Diego	Vincent Mudd
Brigadier General John Paxton, MCRD	Bill Dick
Commander Al Pavich, USN (Ret.), Vietnam Veterans of San Diego	Laurie Black
David Purcell, ENCAD, Inc. (Ret.)	Craig Andrews
Scott Richardson, St. Paul's Cathedral	Cheryl Wilson
James Rotherham, KINTERA, Inc.	Dodie Rotherham
Troy Sears, Next Level Sailing	John Driscoll
Kobi Sethna, Nereus Pharmaceuticals, Inc.	Linda Stirling
Louis Smith, San Diego City Schools	Ronne Froman
Louis Spisto, The Old Globe	Robert Noble
Marc Tarasuck, Marc Tarasuck, AIA & Associates	Suzy Spafford
Richard Tarte, Financial Services (Ret.)	Don Tarte
William Van De Weghe, Klinedinst, Fliehman & McKillop, PC	John Hawkins
Ramona Walker, San Diego Blood Bank	Ed Glazener
Donald Wilkie, Financial Strategies Group	Mickey Flynn
Wes Wilmers, Music & Movies by Mastercraft, Inc.	Chris Sichel
Dan Yates, Regents Bank	Barbara Bry
Mary M. Zoeller, Gyration, Inc.	Barbara Bry

PROGRAMS

An important part of keeping members active and engaged in the life of Rotary revolves around the weekly meetings. The Program Committee worked hard—as always—to find fifty (!) programs that would inform, inspire, stimulate, and entertain members on Thursdays during the year. They succeeded!

◢ President Roscoe and Neil Morgan.

Sports

A. J. Smith, Chargers general manager, and Mark Fabiani, special counsel, addressed Club 33 in July. They spoke about the team, plans for the playoff quest, the club's stadium, and their off-the-field plans, as well as possible new venues for the Chargers.

In January, the Padres came to lunch. Kevin Towers, EVP/general manager, and Jeff Overton, EVP/communications, updated members on Petco Park and prospects for the team in 2004. The keys to Petco were given to the Padres on February 15, and on opening day, April 8, the San Francisco Giants came to town. Good news: the Padres won 4-3!

Jim Brogan, former NBA player, DARE advisor, and color commentator for USD and SDSU, talked about the three common denominators of success: relentless pursuit of goals, courage, and attitude, all necessary elements to achieving career greatness.

◢ Neil Morgan, seated next to Judge Margaret McKeown, enjoyed being surrounded by ladies of Rotary (from left) Janie Davis, a youth exchange student, Patti Roscoe, Barbara Bry, and Peg Eddy.

◢ Patti Roscoe exchanged club flags and banners with a visitor from the Calcutta, India club.

Military

Rotarians heard four programs about various aspects of the military. Commander Ann Phillips spoke about the upcoming commissioning of her ship, the USS *Mustin*, and explained that San Diego had been selected for the commissioning ceremony to honor the local members of the Mustin family, who are retired Navy flag officers. Rotarian Major Andy Hewitt, USMC spoke about his four-month deployment to Iraq and "what you don't see in the media." Rotarians learned that Hewitt is fluent in Farsi. A June program, "What's Ahead in Iraq," featured Major General Jon Gallinetti, commanding general of the Marine Corps Air Base in Miramar, who recently returned from eight months in Iraq as the chief of staff to the military forces running the campaign. Ending on a hopeful note, he stated that Iraq's future as a democracy could be extremely bright with tourism, agriculture, and the second-largest oil reserve on the planet as economic engines.

An inspiring program was Wayne Goodermote's chilling story of surviving five and a half years as a prisoner of war in Viet Nam. In the words of Paul Hartley, Jr., "Wayne understands service in ways the rest of us cannot comprehend."

Bio/Med/Tech

Throughout the year, local representatives from health and medical technology industries educated and informed audiences. Rotarians heard from Dr. Ralph Greenspan of The Neurosciences Institute, who described how genes influence human behavior; Dr. Robert Hertzka, president-elect of the California Medical Association, who spoke about the future of healthcare funding and its options

and alternatives; and Dr. Patrick D. Lyden, director of the UCSD Stroke Center, who updated the audience in the field of stroke prevention. In May, Rotarians learned interesting facts from Michael Welch, MD and Kathleen Sullivan of the American Lung Association. Rotarians learned that the lung's surface, if flattened out, would cover half a tennis court.

Perennial favorites included Jack O'Brian of the Old Globe Theater and Ian Campbell of the San Diego Opera. Tom Fetter, president of the San Diego Zoological Society, shared details about how they watched the Cedar Fire situation closely and described how the condors were moved to the zoo hospital for safekeeping. They were happy to get back to their home unscathed!

Mike Madigan, the new CEO of the proposed Museum of New Americans, founded by Deborah Szekely, the 2001 Ms. San Diego, spoke to Rotarians. Alan Uke, founder of the Midway Museum, reported on the museum's vision for the future, and Chuck Nichols gave an update on the USS *Midway* and its upcoming arrival in San Diego. Dick Sutro's program, "San Diego: Toward Regional Architecture," and Diana Lindsay's on the beauty of the Borrego Desert reinforced how lucky we are to live in "America's Finest City."

Media and Communications

Rotarians enjoyed hearing from various media representatives, including Peter Roussel, director of communications in the Ford and Reagan administrations. Closer to home, programs included Mike Stutz, news director for Channel 10, and Cliff Albert, operations manager for KOGO Radio 600.

The highlight of Staff Appreciation Day was Jane Mitchell, sports interviewer for Channel 4, who marked her eighth season of weekly television programs featuring personalities Ted Williams, Larry Lucchino, and Ryan Klesko. In addition, Leslie Wade of Wade Communications, a leader in the development of the East Village, presented an interesting update.

Fleet Week, October 9

Described by *Sports Illustrated* as "the best closer ever," Trevor Hoffman was the guest speaker for the annual Fleet Week luncheon. In a Q&A

session moderated by Jerry Coleman, Hoffman didn't flinch when asked about his shoulder surgery, his favorite other relievers, and his commitment to family. In fact, he stated that he would be pleased if all three of his sons became school teachers because of their value to society. He described his career highlights as winning the National League,

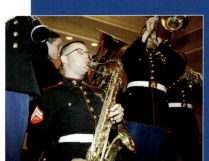

playing in the World Series, beating the Dodgers, and playing ball in the yard with his kids. Over 250 enlisted personnel attended the luncheon.

◢ Top: *President Roscoe with Fleet Week luncheon guests.*

◢ Bottom: *The USMC Band played at the annual Fleet Week luncheon.*

Government Leaders

County assessor Greg Smith was introduced as "one of the—if not THE—best" assessors in California. "If you own it, he will find it and tax it!" was a line from Smith's introduction. In addition to taxing homes and businesses, the county also taxes boats, airplanes, mobile homes, and "animals that are businesses," such as guard dogs and carriage horses. Even our own Shamu receives a tax bill.

George Mitrovich, co-chair (with Rotarian Malin Burnham) of the Good Government Association, spoke about the need to move from a city manager/council form to a strong mayor model of local government. U.S. attorney Carol Lam presented "A Balancing Act" and described the three aspects of her job: legal, administrative, and ceremonial. San Diego Police Chief Bill Landsdowne spoke about "Law Enforcement in Modern America," describing San Diego as a national model for domestic violence programming and community policing.

Additional programs included Dipak Gupta of San Diego State University, who described "The U.S. and the War on Terrorism," and Margaret McKeown, who described her fight as an attorney representing the Seattle-International District Club. She won her case against Rotary International, preventing them from revoking the club's charter for not terminating female members.

Robert Parry, president and CEO of the Federal Reserve Board of San Francisco, explained that San Diego is doing better than the rest of the state. Our unemployment rate in July was 4.7 percent compared to the statewide rate of 7.1 percent. He opined that the local community and the nation are on the way to continued recovery.

Holiday Bowl, December 11

The always popular Holiday Bowl program featured LaVell Edwards, the former BYU coach who brought eleven teams to the Holiday Bowl, now in its twenty-sixth year. In a nail-biting finish, the Washington State Cougars beat the Texas Longhorns 28-20.

Economic Forecast, January

Club 33 kicked off 2004 with the annual economic update. Bill Holland and Al Nevin (who replaced the now-retired Don Bauder) presented "Is the Recovery for Real?" Much discussion revolved around the San Diego real estate market, but other topics included the supermarket strike, trade with China, and how great 2004 should be for the stock market. Their Dow Jones predictions were Holland: 12,000 and Nevin: 11,206. The Dow Jones Industrial Average closed on December 31, 2004, at 10,783.

Holiday Luncheon

▲ Top left: *President Roscoe welcomed her mother to the Holiday Luncheon.*

▲ Top right: *President Roscoe and Ronne Froman enjoyed the Holiday Luncheon.*

▲ Right: *The Rotary Chorus entertained at the annual Holiday Luncheon.*

Sweethearts Day, February 12

Prizes were given for the longest engagement (Natasha Josefowitz and Herman Gadon, twenty years), the most recently married (Katie Fulhorst), marrying the same person twice (Club 33 Executive Assistant Pauline Hill), and the most marriages (Dick Sturgeon, "at least four"). Rick Simas and students from the SDSU Musical Theater MFA program entertained the audience with six songs performed by the students.

▲ Past RI president from Sweden Carl-Wilhelm Stenhammar (2005–2006), Fary Moini of the Golden Triangle Club, and past district governor Steve Brown.

▲ President Roscoe and Barry Lorge (left) welcomed Philippe Lamoise, a visitor from the Torrey Pines Club (La Jolla).

In May, Rotarians were captivated by a panel discussion on the Lost Boys of Sudan. Panelists included Judy Bernstein and Robert Montgomery, SDSU; Kioi Mgubua, a Rotary Scholar studying at USD's Kroc Center for Peace; and Benson Deng, one of the Lost Boys of Sudan, Rotaract Club. In 1988, 20,000 boys, aged five to eleven years, were forced to leave their homes because of ethnic and religious wars in Sudan. Of the 3,000 boys who were resettled in the U.S., one hundred are in San Diego.

THE ROAST

Rascal Roscoe Gets Roasted

President Patti "Rascal" Roscoe's fervent wishes for an understated roast were completely ignored, and the show went on in grand style. Several past presidents in drag marched in to the sound of "I Am Woman." The Navy Band played "76 Trombones," "The

▲ Top left: Patti at her roast with past president Frank.

▲ Top right: Past presidents, back row (from left): Bill Beamer and Ben Clay; front row (from left): G. T. Frost, Jr., Patti Roscoe, George Carter Jessop, and Shelly Brockett.

▲ Left: The past presidents honored Patti amid a sea of confetti.

◢ The U.S. Navy Band (Southwest Region) played at the roast.

◢ The past presidents honored Patti Roscoe at her roast.

Star-Spangled Banner," and "Anchors Aweigh." A wonderful video, scripted and produced by Barry Lorge, portrayed glimpses from Patti's past. Katherine Kennedy sung her rendition of "My Favorite Things," and Patti's BFFs shared their personal experiences with Patti accompanied by video clips from appropriate movies. Past president Frank Arrington presented Patti with the past president's pin and the year ended on many hilarious and high notes!

Salute to Local Heroes, January 29

Local heroes were presented by DA Bonnie Dumanis, SDPD Chief Bill Landsdowne, and San Diego County Sheriff Bill Kolender. Each year, the stories amaze and inspire. An eleven-year-old headed off a potential kidnapper, a bystander took gunshots and baseball bat blows to the head while rescuing a victim, a trio fought an armed robber at a casino, a citizen tackled an attacker who had grabbed an officer's weapon, and a citizen ensured the safety of an entire school against a car thief. Rotarians applauded those efforts which resulted in a safer environment for all.

◢ Chet Lathrop received congratulations from President Roscoe on his fifteenth year as Club 33's executive director.

Timeline

August 7, 2003 — One program featured John DeBello, director and co-producer of the cult classic *Attack of the Killer Tomatoes*, celebrating its twenty-fifth anniversary.

October 25–28, 2003 — Cedar Fire: 280,278 acres, 2,820 buildings, and 15 deaths

October 2003–March 2004 — Southern California Grocery Strike

April 8, 2004 — First game at Petco Park. Padres 4, Giants 3. Rah!

Mr. San Diego: George Gildred, September 25

Born in the old Scripp's Clinic, George Gildred has always been knee-deep in making San Diego what it has become. Professional football, the stadium, several organizations at SDSU and UCSD, the Zoological Society, the SeaWorld Research Center, the San Diego Chamber of Commerce, and ConVis are a few of the organizations that are richer for Gildred's selfless involvement and support. In addition, he served as the honorary Chilean Consul and as the 1972–1973 president of Club 33.

▲ President Patti Roscoe and George Gildred were surrounded by (from left) a friend, Bert Wahlen, Dick Murphy, Bruce Moore, and Mark Trotter.

▲ George Gildred (Mr. San Diego) and Mayor Dick Murphy.

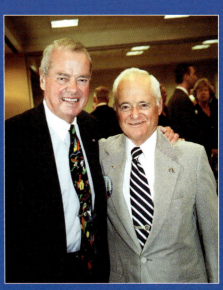

▲ George Gildred (Mr. San Diego) and Paul Hartley, Jr.

▲ Past presidents (from left) Bruce Moore, Ross Pyle, George Gildred, Mort Jorgensen, and Jim Haugh.

CHAPTER FOUR

Thomas R. Vecchione, MD

2004–2005

" When you make someone feel better, you've performed a real service of Rotary. "

◢ CHANGE OF COMMAND

July 1, 2004 was a typical near-perfect San Diego day for Dr. Thomas R. Vecchione's inaugural meeting. The theme for the year, "Celebrating 100 Years of Rotary," was announced along with the reminder about District 5340's gala on July 18 to celebrate Rotary International's centennial.

Although a member of Rotary since 1980, Rotarians learned that Vecchione's earliest introduction to Rotary occurred during his high school days in Ohio. As one of the founding physicians of the Mercy Outreach Surgical Team (MOST), he spoke fondly and passionately about the strong connection between Rotary clubs—both in Mexico and Club 33—and MOST. In fact, Rotary support of a surgical project in Mexicali, Mexico, thirty-five years ago was what prompted Vecchione to join Club 33.

Duly installed by Mayor Dick Murphy, the new president introduced the Board of Directors and summarized goals for the upcoming year. In his remarks, Vecchione recalled Satchel Paige, who said, "If you don't know where you're goin', you might end up goin' someplace else." Well, Vecchione knew exactly where he was goin'. His priorities were taking healthcare to indigent children, youth education through Camp Enterprise, interaction with middle schools and Monarch High School, and Rotary recruitment and retention.

▴ President Tom Vecchione.

▴ President Vecchione and Geri Ann Warnke.

▴ Tom and Sylvia Vecchione celebrated the Rotary International Centennial at the Hotel del Coronado in July.

Increasing fines was not overlooked. President Vecchione cut to the quick and levied a $250 fine on Martha Dennis for her appearance on the cover of a local magazine. The breathtaking fines started by Frank Arrington continued during the year. By January, President Vecchione was all warmed up with a fine of $2,005 (!) to Robert Horsman. On March 3, he fined a deceased member of Club 33, and on March 10, the cookie-toting Girl Scouts bore the brunt! There was no stopping his fining scalpel and it was all in good fun!

Rotary International's Centennial Celebration

During Rotary International's centennial year, several special events occurred. On the Rotary's actual birthday, February 23, 2005, Vecchione could not be present in Chicago, but he celebrated in Uruapan, Michoacán, Mexico, with the local Rotary Club (nineteen members strong), where over 300 children had been surgically helped by the MOST team. In April, Rotarians and ten special MOST children joined the opening ceremonies at Petco Park to view the beautiful Flag Court established by District 5340 and enjoy the game. The June Rotary International Convention in Chicago included a Rotary history display from its first project of a public restroom in downtown Chicago to the thousands of Rotary service projects around the world today.

SERVICE ABOVE SELF

Early in the Rotary new year, the World Community Service Committee announced that work days for the Otay/Tijuana school projects would take place monthly between August and December. Fish Across the Border celebrated its tenth anniversary and, thanks to Bob Fletcher and his committee of fisherpersons, hungry families in Ensenada continue to benefit from its largesse.

The MOST team traveled to Tijuana in October and Tula, Hidalgo, in November and February. To date, over 5,000 special children have had transformative surgeries.

Dr. Sergio Hidalgo Ramirez, director of the General Hospital in Tijuana, may have said it best: "To give without receiving is a divine act carried out by dedicated people." In April, it was announced that the Tijuana surgeries would take place at Hospital Ingles.

A spring program featured Club 33-er and past president Bill McDade's wonderful slideshow of all the good that is being done in Malawi. He proudly reported that a four-wheel-drive vehicle was purchased to transport children in need to the hospital in Malawi. Other projects continued that supported Monarch High School, After School Tennis, and the Rotary Youth Leadership Awards (RYLA).

▲ Right: Sylvia Vecchione (front row, second from right) with MOST staff and volunteers.

▲ Below left: Sylvia and Tom Vecchione at a MOST clinic.

▲ Below right: President Vecchione with a MOST patient and parent.

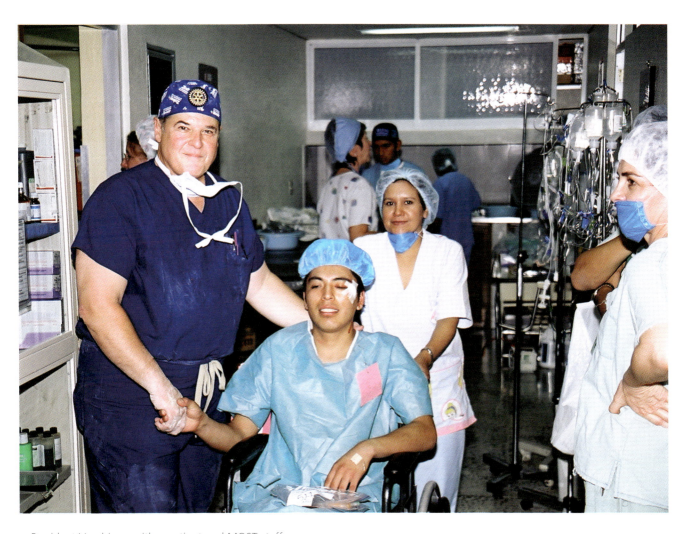

◢ President Vecchione with a patient and MOST staff.

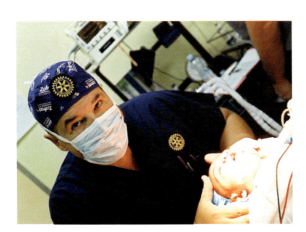

◢ President Vecchione with a patient, just finishing surgery.

◢ President Vecchione with a patient.

Thirtieth Camp Enterprise, April 14

Chaired by Judge Pete Bowie, speakers included Rotary's own entrepreneurs Chris Cramer, Karl Strauss Breweries; Mike Morton, the Brigantine Restaurants; Lorin Stewart, Old Town Trolley; Diana Venable, D&D Estate Liquidators; and Wes Wilmers, Music & Movies by Mastercraft.

▲ *Diana Venable was a Camp Enterprise speaker.*

MEMBERSHIP

Fellowship, Camaraderie, and Engagement

Jack White gave $500,000 to the San Diego Fire Department for the lifesaving emergency treatment he received during his heart attack. Chief Jeff Bowman stated that it was the largest private donation the department had ever received—what a stunning thank-you! Jack's response was, "Service to community is above self. It's an old Rotarian phrase that I try to live by." No question there!

Patti Roscoe received an Outstanding Achievement Award from the District Council, and the Circle of Life Award was presented to President Vecchione. Will Newbern and Andy Hewitt swam the Hudson River in New York City and raised $4,135. A celebration of Neil Morgan was held at the campus of UCSD, and Chet Lathrop marked his fifteenth year as executive director of the Rotary Club of San Diego.

Rotarians in the News

Several busy members of Club 33 were asked to lead organizational boards, including Joyce Gattas, Convention and Visitors Bureau Executive Committee. Joe Craver and Phil Blair were also named to the committee. Other members supporting organizations included Cheryl Wilson, California Association of Homes and Services for the Aging; Geri Warnke, Sidney Kimmel Cancer Center; Phil Blair and Marlee Ehrenfeld, NTC Foundation; Mike Murphy, San Diego Chamber of Commerce; Bruce Blakley, The San Diego Foundation; and Bill Kolender, who was named president of the California State Sheriffs' Association.

Additional Rotarians serving on boards included Carol Wallace, United Way of San Diego County; Bill Dopp, Seabury Institute, an Episcopalian seminary; Robert Horsman, BRAVO! San Diego Board; and Ed Chaplin, Board of Examiners, Malcolm Baldrige National Quality Award.

Appointments

Governor Arnold Schwarzenegger appointed Bill Kolender and Andrew Poat to the Mental Health Services Oversight and Accountability Commission, created by Proposition 63, and Sandy Purdon to the Boating and Waterways Commission. Sarah Lamade was appointed to the board of the city's data processing corporation. Paul

Downey was appointed to the White House Conference on Aging.

Awards

Chris Cramer and his wife, Kirsten, were honored with The Spirit of Life Award by the City of Hope. Ian Campbell received the 2004 Wolfensohn Award presented annually by the Sydney (Australia) University Graduates Union of North America. Bill Kolender was selected as the first honoree of the Public Safety Leaders Award, sponsored by the Miramar College Foundation. Robert Horsman received the American Jewish Committee's 2005 Community Service Award, San Diego Chapter. Larry Shea was a recipient of the University of San Diego's highest honor, the Author E. Hughes Career Achievement Award. Jim Mulvaney and his wife, Ruth, were honored at the twenty-seventh anniversary of the Mingei Museum for their longtime support. Malin Burnham received a Lifetime Achievement Award at the Entrepreneur of the Year Program in San Diego. Jo Dee Jacob received the Executive Excellence Award from Nonprofit Management Solutions for her achievement, performance, and leadership of the Girl Scouts. Joe Jessop was inducted into the San Diego Hall of Champions.

San Diego State University, represented by President Stephen Weber, received a Friends of Balboa Park Millennium Award.

Business Honors

Linda Stirling and her team were among "America's Top 50 Advisors," named by *Registered Rep* magazine. Thella Bowens and Sarah Lamade were winners in *San Diego Business Journal*'s 2004 "Women Who Mean Business," and Robert Horsman was inducted into Junior Achievement's San Diego Business Hall of Fame.

Fun Times

Not known for "all work and no play," Rotarians somehow managed to find time in their busy schedules to connect with fellow members and their guests on regular occasions. In July, fifty members and guests from Club 33 attended the Centennial Gala. The annual Day at the Races brought big fun to attendees, but small change to their pockets. September was all about the water with the annual Sail and BBQ at the San Diego Yacht Club and the annual Club 33 fishing trip. Golfers in the group enjoyed outings in August, when Golf Committee Chair Bob Mattis won the intraclub tourney, and again in November. In June, six members played in the tournament at Eastgate Country Club. The A Team, made up of Bob Mattis, Guy Maddox, Tom Creamer, and Rod Eales, earned six points and finished in first place. The B Team of Lou Wax and Mickey Flynn earned two points.

PROGRAMS

Staff Appreciation Day in April was simply out of this world. James Benson, founder/president and CEO of SpaceDev, described his involvement in last year's historic SpaceShipOne, mankind's first commercial space flight.

New Members

NAME	PRIMARY SPONSOR
Scott Alevy, San Diego Regional Chamber of Commerce	Karen Hutchens
Kobe Bogaert, Spring Strategies	Richard Walker
Robert Borgman, First National Bank	Ed Fahlen
Daniel P. Brogan, Smith Consulting Architects	Dan Yates
Jeffrey Brown, San Diego Fire Chief	Peg Eddy
Mario Bourdon, PhD, La Jolla Institute of Molecular Medicine	Barbara Bry
Richard Carr, TEC International	Barbara Bry
Sheryl Charleston Bilbrey, Better Business Bureau	Paul Palmer
Phillip Currie, Shoreline Partners, LLC	Dan Yates
Laura Stanley DeMarco, Nicholas-Applegate Capital Management (Ret.)	Sharon Hilliard
Marye Anne Fox, UCSD	Natasha Josefowitz
Richard J. Freeman, Padres	Bill Fiss
Randy Frisch, *San Diego Union Tribune*	Marilyn Creson
Jim Groen, Charco Construction	Paul Woo
Matthew Hom, MD, Hom Medical Group, Inc.	Gene Rumsey, Jr., MD
Charles B. Hope, Jr., Hope Engineering	Paul J. Hartley, Jr.
Theodore M. Kanatas, Manchester Grand Hyatt	Patti Roscoe
Edwin Kofler, San Diego Center for Children	Ben Haddad
Lewis Linson, SAIC (Ret.)	George Harris
Mary E. Lyons, University of San Diego	Ky Snyder
Michael McDowell, California Comfort Systems	Paul J. Hartley, Jr.
Mark McKinnon, McKinnon Properties, Inc.	John Hawkins
Ailene McManus, Lucky Line Products, Inc.	Ed Kitrosser
Armon Mills, *San Diego Business Journal*	Fred Baranowski
Joe Moeller, International Sports Council	Ky Synder
Victor Ramsauer, Levitz, Zacks & Ciceric	Richard Walker
Mike Richardson, Sherpa Alliance	Joanne Pastula
Garry Ridge, WD-40	Paul Hering
Jeanne Schmelzer, Netzel Associates	Clark Siebrand
Daniel Shea, Donovan's Steak & Chop House	Bill Dick
Beverly Siligmueller, The Alford Group	Dave Mitchell
Susan Snow, Maxim Systems, Inc.	Dan Yates
Claudio Stemberger, Et Lux Lucet	Chet Lathrop
Steven Sullivan, Sullivan International Group, Inc.	Richard Walker
Lucinda Trowbridge, Combined Health Agencies	Janie Davis
Dee Van Horne, Add Web Marketing Services	Chet Lathrop

Rotarians of the Quarter

Kenny Jones   Richard Walker

Bill Ward   Doug Arbon, MD

▲ *President Vecchione with Bill Ward, a Rotarian of the Quarter.*

Foreign/Exotic Make-ups

During the year, traveling Rotarians made up meetings in a variety of exotic and foreign locations. Travelers included Marc Tarasuck, Kyoto-South, Japan; Dennis Vanier, Bombay, India; Linda Moore, Pembroke, Bermuda; Guy Maddox, Ensenada, Mexico; and Karen Green, Queenstown, New Zealand. George Carter Jessop made up a meeting in St. Petersburg, Russia, and Dave Purcell attended a meeting in Brasov, Romania. Additional make-ups were recorded by Jim Hughes, DePertuis-Durance-Cadenet, France; Tracy Lau, St. Tropez, France; Bill Van De Weghe, Mechelen Opsinjoor, Belgium; Dave Purcell, Siena, Italy; Bink Cook, Genova, Italy; Kobe Bogaert, Kavlinge, Sweden; and Marten Barry, Munich, Feiedensengal, Germany.

Make-ups occurred aboard many ships on the high seas, including Lyle Butler, *River Explorer*, from Budapest to Amsterdam; Darlene Davies, *Norwegian Wind*; Chris Sichel, *Spirit*, Carnival Cruise Line; Lewis Linson, *Mercury*, Celebrity Cruises; Newt Pollock, *Queen Mary 2*; Natasha Josefowitz and Herman Gadon, *Statendam*; Chuck Duddles, *Princess*; Bill Herrin, *Ryndam* and *River Explorer*, from Budapest to Amsterdam; and Jo Briggs, *Seven Seas Mariner*.

In Memoriam

Hewes A. Bell

John Benson

J. Dallas Clark

James F. Clement, PhD (Honorary Member)

Alex De Bakcsy

Frederick Kunzel

Roy W. Potter

Ray A. Robbins

Bill Stephens

Gerry F. Wilson

Board of Directors, 2004–2005

Thomas R. Vecchione, MD, President

James M. Hughes, President-elect

Suzanne "Suzy" Spafford, Secretary

Daryl E. "Debbie" Day, Treasurer

Patricia L. "Patti" Roscoe, Past President

H. L. "Hal" Gardner

Wayne K. Goodermote

Richard M. Green, DPM

Stanford F. Hartman, Jr.

Albert T. Harutunian III

Barry S. Lorge

Robert G. Russell, Jr.

Bonnie Schwartz

Nancy Scott

Diana D. Venable

Grotarian Events

In addition to getting to know about Rotary and mingling with other members, Grotarians enjoyed an August picnic and Starlight Theater performance of *The Music Man* and visits to the Humane Society and Sharp Hospital. A tour of the USS *Ronald Reagan* and a concert in Tijuana offered something for just about everyone.

Health Programs

President Vecchione had been chief of staff at Children's Hospital from 1986 to 1988 and he invited Blair Sadler, the current president/CEO of Children's Hospital & Health Center, to talk about the hospital's fifty-year history in San Diego. Dr. John Reed, the president/CEO of the Burnham Institute, updated Club 33 about one of the world's top-rated life-science research organizations. Dr. Peter Ferrell, the CEO of ResMed Corporation, shared information about sleep disorders and the importance of a good night's sleep for everyone's general health.

Sports

Popular sports-themed programs included ESPN broadcaster Jon Miller, Padres' Mark Loretta at the Fleet Week luncheon in October, and in March, infielder Mark Grant, who played second base for the Padres. The December Holiday Bowl program featured highlights of the 1984 game when number-one BYU beat Michigan for the national championship. Attending the meeting were Robbie Boscoe (quarterback), and Leon White (linebacker), members of the 1984 BYU team.

Local and Regional Updates

Club 33 welcomed a variety of representatives from businesses, agencies, and organizations, including the San Diego Regional Airport, the Humane Society, San Diego Fire Rescue Department, San Diego Gas & Electric, CCDC, and the San Diego River Restoration Project. Executives from GenProbe, WD-40, Qualcomm, and The San Diego Foundation (celebrating their thirtieth anniversary) also contributed valuable updates.

A March program titled "The Big Picture" brought a fascinating conversation with Dr. Derrick Cartwright from the San Diego Art Museum, John Petersen from the Timken Museum of Art, and Dr. Hugh Davies from the Museum of Contemporary Art.

Dr. Otto Mower of The Bishop's School and Frieder Seible and Richard Atkinson, both of UCSD, brought programs regarding their educational institutions.

More programs contributed to Club 33's knowledge base. Past district governor Steve Brown described his work in Afghanistan and Robert Swan talked about his walk on both the North and South poles. Rotarians also enjoyed programs featuring Scott (son of Ken, the "One Minute Manager") Blanchard, Assistant Attorney General Thomas Sansonetti, and Kyoto Laureate Allan C. Kay.

"Luann" cartoonist Greg Evans and Stephen J. Cannell, writer, author, and producer, both presented entertaining programs. Rev. Barry Minkow shared details of his life as a swindler and subsequent eight-year prison term, followed by his career as an undercover investigator and, ultimately, as a born-again pastor. Other programs included Nissan Design America and Accredited Home Lenders, Inc., as well as information on cyber crime and the Orange County bankruptcy situation.

Holiday Luncheon

The annual Holiday Luncheon featured two highlights. Lieutenant Colonel Andy Hewitt, who was serving in Iraq, sent a poignant "Christmas Letter from Iraq," read by Clark Anthony. Past president and longtime Rotary chorus director Homer Peabody directed the chorus and audience in holiday favorites. Sadly, it would be Peabody's final holiday program, as he passed away in December 2005.

———————————

Economic Forecast, January 6, 2004

January 6 brought the annual economic update with Bill Holland (San Diego's "Voice of Wall Street") and Jim Welsh (Welsh Money Management). Their year-end predictions were Holland: 13,000, and Welsh: 10,200. The Dow Jones Industrial Average closed at 10,718 on December 30, 2005.

———————————

Sweethearts Day

The popular Sweethearts Day program brought a real treat from Ian Campbell and the San Diego Opera Ensemble with their presentation, "Love Songs in English."

———————————

Visitors

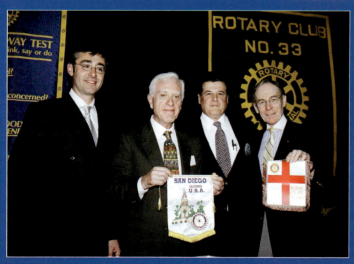

▲ *Rotarians from Milan with President Vecchione.*

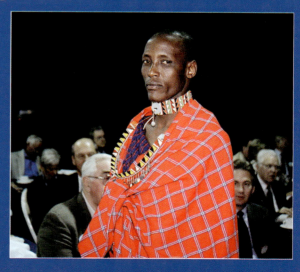

▲ *A visiting Rotarian in colorful garb.*

St. Patrick's Day

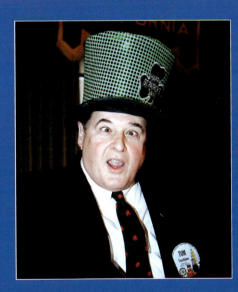

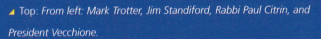

▲ Top: *From left: Mark Trotter, Jim Standiford, Rabbi Paul Citrin, and President Vecchione.*

▲ Middle right: *Paul Hartley III and Paul Hartley, Jr. celebrated St. Patrick's Day.*

▲ Above: *President Tom O'Vecchione at the St. Patrick's Day meeting.*

▲ Right: *Guest speaker General Paxton.*

THE ROAST

Roasting Tom

Going down in history as a "HUGE HIT," this roast had it all… from thirty past presidents in scrubs to the Pope (a.k.a. Frank Arrington), "appearances" by Dean Martin and Dr. Frankenstein, and appropriate movie clips and early photos of Tom and his family. Bill McDade shared photos and stories of Tom's work which transformed the lives of his littlest patients. The Club 33 Singers performed the Barry Lorge rendition of "That's Amore Vecchion-e."

Few people exhibit "service above self" more effectively or dramatically than Club 33's Tom Vecchione. Several heartfelt standing ovations interrupted the proceedings. The meeting concluded with Patti Roscoe's presentation of the past president's pin, a backpack, jacket, and light tent! Go in peace, past president Tom!

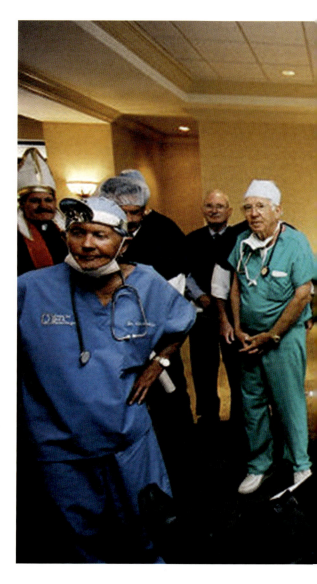

◢ Top photo: Tom was wheeled into his roast under the watchful eyes of doctors/ past presidents.

◢ Past presidents honored Tom (back row, center).

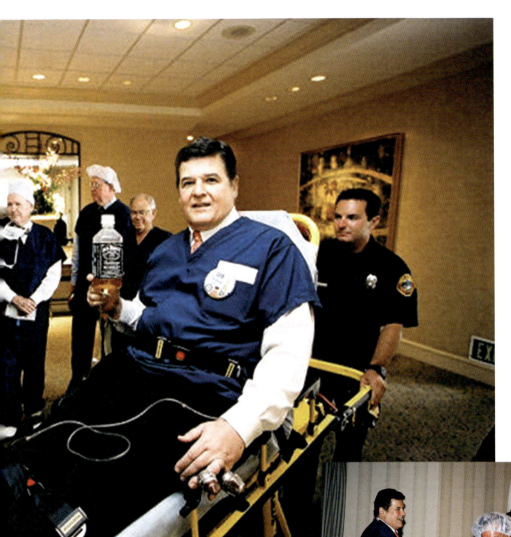

▲ Past presidents (from left) Norm Roberts, Bruce Moore, and Jim Haugh enjoyed the roast.

▲ Bill McDade joined in the roasting Tom fest.

▲ The Pope (a.k.a. Frank Arrington) and Tom Vecchione at Tom's roast.

▲ Past president Fred Baranowski congratulated Tom.

▲ G. T. Frost, Jr. (far left) and Bert Wahlen helped roast Tom.

Mr. San Diego: Cecil Steppe, August 12, 2004

Almost a native San Diegan, Cecil Steppe came to San Diego at the age of one, went to San Diego High School, and worked as a San Diego County probation officer for thirty-five years. He ultimately headed the Department of Health and Human Services. Currently, Steppe serves as president/CEO of the San Diego Urban League. The Speaker of the Day was Neil Morgan, who recalled his early days in San Diego and the importance of institutions such as the Globe Theaters, the La Jolla Playhouse, and the local university system as emerging economic engines for the region.

———————

Fleet Week, October 14

Chair of the Day Bob Russell introduced the speaker, All-Star Mark Loretta, who had a spectacular year as second baseman for the Padres. Loretta talked about his career in baseball in general and with the Padres specifically. The young team had strong talent, especially rookie players Kahlil Greene, Sean Burroughs, and pitcher Jake Peavy. A special treat was an email from Club 33's own Andy Hewitt, currently serving in Fallujah, Iraq.

———————

Salute to Local Heroes, January 13

At the Salute to Local Heroes, Sheriff Bill Kolender presented Nina Conner, whose call of suspicious activity in a residence led to a major marijuana bust including the shut-down of twenty-eight residential marijuana farms. Police Chief Bill Landsdowne introduced Ahmed Omar and Juan Lopez, who had saved a woman and her child from being stabbed by the woman's husband. DA Bonnie Dumanis told about Dominic Camacho, who chased a fleeing suspect and held him until police arrived. The suspect was armed and wanted for two attempted murders among other charges. A ten-year-old boy was honored for turning in his drug-using mother to local police after she forced him to assist in the burglary of a neighbor's house. President Vecchione presented a special award to Alma Ditty, who gets in her car each evening to drive around and look for suspicious activity. Several times she has stopped a crime in progress and the SDPD officers know to take her calls, as her information is accurate.

———————

Dedication of Petco Park, April 8, 2005

The Rotary Flag Court at Petco Park honored the one-hundredth anniversary of Rotary International and was celebrated in a big way by both Club 33 and members of the Rotary clubs in District 5340.

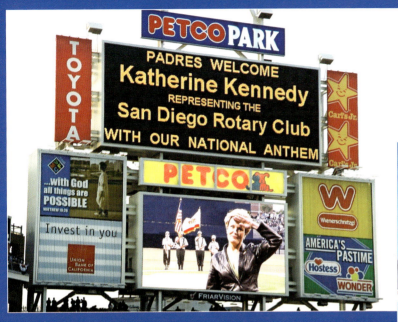

◄ Katherine Kennedy sang the National Anthem at the dedication.

◄ From left: Past president Patti Roscoe, Executive Director Chet Lathrop, Sandi Rimer (District 5340), and Cliff Dochterman at the dedication.

◄ Pat and Hugh Carter at the Rotary Flag Court dedication festivities.

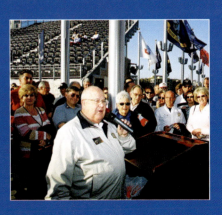

◄ The crowds had a great time at the dedication of the Rotary Flag Court.

◄ The Rotary Flag Court at Petco Park honored the one-hundredth anniversary of Rotary International.

◄ Cliff Dochterman at the dedication.

CHAPTER FIVE

James M. Hughes
2005–2006

"I'm an ordinary guy among extraordinary people."

CHANGE OF COMMAND

On Bastille Day in 2005, almost-past-mayor Dick Murphy administered the oath of office to almost-president James M. Hughes. In his remarks, Murphy said, "Jim is a person who personifies Rotary." He went on to extol Hughes' perfect attendance of over fourteen years, his active involvement in over half of the committees, and his role as landlord for the Club 33 office.

Not one to rest on his laurels, Hughes outlined his plans for the year. His priorities were to use members' time wisely, cut down introductions and announcements to one minute each, and—most importantly—give priority to service. Focal points included plans to determine a Major Community Project, complete a meaningful Rotary Centennial Project, and launch "Rotarians at Work Day" as an annual activity, as well as enhance the hundreds of other activities and events of Club 33. Club 33 also looked forward to hosting the Assembly for all of Rotary International in 2006.

Of course, fines were not ignored and members ponied up in a big way. At his first meeting, the new president dinged John Hawkins, Will Newbern, and Andy Hewitt for a total of $1,250. In September, Hughes hit Vince Mudd up in absentia, proving that you don't even have to be present to be fined!

Deborah Lindholm, founder of the Foundation for Women, presented the first program of the year on micro-credit. Dedicated to nurturing and educating women around the globe, especially the poor, the homeless, and the terminally ill, the program could not have been more appropriate—an inspiring start for another outstanding Club 33 year.

SERVICE ABOVE SELF

The Rotary International Centennial created a "grand call" for big projects around the world. District 5340 and Club 33 partnered to create the Rotary Flag Court at Petco Park. Twenty-two flagpoles were erected, all paid for by Rotarians. Three of the poles bear the names of San Diego Rotary, John Berry, and James M. Hughes.

The World Community Service Project, led by Dick Jackson, was busy building a Red Cross Ambulance Center in Tijuana. The dedicated team assembled monthly and included Peter Duncan, Gary Gould, Michael Kenny, Steve LaDow, Norbert Sanders, Jerry Van Ert, and Wes Wilmers.

On September 1, the club officiated at the graduation of two women from Monarch High School, both of whom were heading off to college. What a triumph for them!

Members of the Rotary Club of Tehuacan, Mexico, attended a November meeting to thank San Diego Rotary and the Mercy Outreach Surgical Team for the recent mission that treated 293 patients. The attention was well-deserved by physicians Doug Arbon, Tom Vecchione, and father-and-son doctors Gene Rumsey, Sr. and Gene Rumsey, Jr., as well as Bill and Barbara Ward and several other medical professionals in Club 33.

In January, Bob Fletcher led the sixteenth annual

Fish Across the Border project in Ensenada, Mexico. A pack of Rotarians follow Fletcher to Ensenada each year, including past president Mike Morton.

In February, Jay Arnett was awarded the Gene Rumsey Trophy for an eighty-seven-pound tuna caught during the annual Club 33 fishing trip. February 18 was another "Work Day in Tijuana."

The last Saturday in April was the inaugural "Rotarians at Work Day." Club 33 marshaled over 200 members and more than one hundred others to give a day of service. Eighteen local projects were identified, including painting and planting at Veterans Village and painting at St. Paul's Senior Center. In addition, members were busy at the Barrio Logan Community Clinic Health Fair and the San Diego Rescue Mission Emergency Homeless Shelter. Another group used lots of elbow grease and spruced up the outside of an elderly woman's small cottage.

◂ Rotarians at Work Day.

San Diego Rotary leads the world in projects successfully completed at the annual Rotary at Work Day. Space limits mentioning by name the hundreds in the club who participate.

May 11 found a bunch of Rotarians and some offspring (future Rotarians, perhaps?) at the Community Care Center and St. Paul's Park. They painted walls and touched up the sandbox and play equipment. Participants included Mark Allan, Pat Caughey, Patrick Goddard, Sue Honeycutt, Terri Hutton, Debi Ives, Newt Pollock, Cheryl Rhode (and daughter, Megan), Marc Tarasuck, Peter Van Horne (and son, Sam), and Bob Witty.

Although Rotarians do not serve for honor and recognition, several members were honored this year for a variety of "Service Above Self" efforts. The RI Service Above Self Award was presented to Dr. Tom Vecchione for his renowned work with the MOST team. Cheryl Wilson was presented with the District Award for her "Don't Wait, Vaccinate" Program. The Bob Cleator, Sr. Award went to Ray McKewon for dedicated service to Camp Enterprise. Phil Blair and Mel Katz were honored by the Copley Family YMCA and KSWB Cares for Kids. George Carter Jessop received an Essence of Life Award by Elderhelp of San Diego, and Katherine Kennedy and Robert Horsman served as co-chairs for the annual Mercy Ball.

President Hughes' speaker's gift each week was a personalized framed certificate indicating

Camp Enterprise, March 2–4

Chairman Chris Cramer started with a bang, drawing the largest crowd of students ever: one hundred! The kick-off Rotary luncheon was led by Faux Riche Brian Lange, who demonstrated what it was like to have money to burn and showed off his jet, homes, cars, and assorted "bling." There was only one problem—the students would need to develop a business that was incredibly successful to result in all those "details."

▲ Brian Lange at the Camp Enterprise kick-off luncheon.

Auction for Scholarships

▲ Jim Hughes read the winners of the annual opportunity drawing he sponsors for the Diana Venable Scholarship Fund.

that Rotary was selecting a Major Community Project and a contribution was being made in the name of the speaker. Due to the challenges of naming a specific project, the goals for the 2005–2006 year were not finalized and the funds were turned over to The Diana Venable Scholarship Fund.

MEMBERSHIP

Fellowship, Camaraderie, and Engagement

Beginning with his first meeting, President Hughes vowed to "use members' time well" and focus on important service projects and goals that would affect members in a positive way. Major goals were to begin the transition from paper-dependent communication to electronic methods, such as email and the website, and the remodeling of the Rotary offices. These were multi-year projects and President Hughes stayed involved with them long after his term ended.

Rotary Fun Times

Commencing with the annual Day at the Races (big fun, little wins) in August and ending with the Club 33 Tennis Tournament in March (won by Vern Aguirre), Rotarians appreciated those times when they could relax and enjoy each other's company. A special occasion for Hughes was the opportunity to meet the winners of the San Diego Rotary Race at Del Mar. Like presidents before him, Hughes presented roses and champagne to the owners of the winning horse.

Other social events included the annual Sail and BBQ, a Rotary RV Rally in Borrego Springs, and the Paul Harris Gala at the San Diego Air & Space Museum. In October, golfers Bonnie Schwartz and Bob Mattis captured wins at the San Diego Country Club.

Members Named to Lead Organizations

Richard Ledford was named chair of the Board of Directors for the San Diego/Imperial Counties Chapter of the American Red Cross, and Sandy Purdon was elected chair of the California Boating and Waterways Commission. Ronne Froman was sworn in as the mayor's chief operating officer on January 1, 2006. Bruce Blakley assumed the presidency of The San Diego Foundation.

Awards and Honors Go to Club 33 Members

Each year, Rotarians are among hundreds of people honored in San Diego for various activities, and this year was no exception.

Jo Dee Jacob received one of the first fellowships for Nonprofit Leadership Awards granted by the Harvard Business School Alumni Club of San Diego and The San Diego Foundation. The San Diego Multiple Sclerosis Society honored UCSD Chancellor Marye Anne Fox and presidents Mary Lyons (USD) and Stephen Weber (SDSU) at the "Diamonds of Academia" event. Joanne Pastula, president of Junior Achievement of San Diego/Imperial Counties, received the 2005 Karl Flemke Pioneer Achievement Award during the Junior Achievement Global Leadership Conference in Toronto. Malin Burnham received the 2005 Robert Breitbard Award, which recognizes those who have furthered sports in San Diego County. Mark Trotter and his wife, Jean, were honored at the consecration of the Trotter Chapel and Music Center of the First Methodist Church in Mission Valley.

▲ SDSU President and Club 33 member Stephen Weber, Joyce Gattas, and President Hughes. Weber noted his tenth anniversary at SDSU.

Bonnie Schwartz and her design team received an international Crystal Award of Excellence from The Communicators and an international Gold Award from The Summit Creative Awards for their recent work. In December, Rod Eales' SDA Security Systems, Inc. received a 2005 Family Business of the Year Award in the "Medium Owned" category. The awards are presented annually by the University of San Diego's Family Business Forum in conjunction with the *San Diego Business Journal*. Rich DeBolt, San Diego Van and Storage, received the Mayflower Joyce Derrick Award. Bill McColl was one of three San Diegans honored as "California Basketball High School Player of the Year" in the over one-hundred-year history of the award.

The *San Diego Business Journal* named Charlie Van Vechten one of the "40 under Forty" and Joyce Glazer and Ronne Froman were among the 2005 "Women Who Mean Business."

PROGRAMS

There is nothing that San Diego Rotary does better than its programs, and 2005–2006 was no exception. The first program of President Hughes' term was on July 7 with Neil "The Voice of San Diego" Morgan. San Diego-centric programs served to bring members up to date on a variety of issues affecting this region. Members heard from Duane Roth, CONNECT; the SeaWorld general manager, who brought some "special guests"; La Jolla Playhouse; KPBS; and Rotary's own Dr. Stephen Weber, on his tenth anniversary as president of SDSU. From the city, Rotarians heard updates from Mayor Jerry Sanders, City Attorney Mike Aguirre, and Dr. Carl Cohn, new superintendent of San Diego City Schools.

Kelly Perdue, the survivor of Donald Trump's *The Apprentice*, spoke to Club 33

New Members

NAME	PRIMARY SPONSOR
Craig Blower, Reuben H. Fleet Science Center	Martha Dennis
Mary Braunwarth, Mercy Hospital Foundation	Tom Vecchione
Daniel P. Brogan, Smith Consulting Architects	Dan Yates
Mike Caruso, Booz Allen Hamilton	Paul J. Hartley, Jr.
Kevin Clark, Southwest Hospitality Associates	Ed Chaplin
Laura DeMarco, Institutional Investments (Ret.)	Sharon Hilliard
Matthew Engel, Cabrillo Hoist	John Hawkins
Walter Fegley, Reno Construction, Inc.	Dan Yates
Tom Fleming, San Diego Data Processing Corporation	Mary Zoeller
Steve Francis, AMN Healthcare	Phil Blair
Debbie Giaquinta, The Charter School of San Diego	Jeremiah Doran
Robert Guarnotta, AIG	Paul J. Hartley, Jr.
Patrick Kane, C. B. Richard Ellis	Hal Gardner
Michael Kenny, Joseph P. Kenny & Associates	Chet Lathrop
Steven Libman, La Jolla Playhouse	Geri Warnke
David MacVean, Collins MacVean, LLC	Mike Collins
Valerie McCartney, Pepsi Co.	Richard Walker
Joe Mannino, North Bay Association	Chuck Pretto
Lisa Mednick, Union Bank of California	Ron Kendrick
Robert Morton, Farmer (Ret.)	Chuck Pretto
Tim Murphy, Elite Racing	John Reid
Craig Nelson, First National Bank	Larry Clapper
Cheryl Rhode, West Rhode & Roberts	Dodie Rotherham
Michael Robinson, Sherpa Alliance & TEC	Joanne Pastula
Dana M. Sabraw, U.S. District Court	Rudi Brewster
Kirk Sanfillipo, Port of San Diego Harbor Police Department	Bill Kolender
Doug Sawyer, United Way of San Diego County	Fred Baranowski
Ed Smith, Jr., Plaza Financial Group, Inc.	Joe Davies
Russell Strenk, Boy Scouts of America	Steve Mueller
Mark Stuart, Zoological Society of San Diego	Chuck Bieler
Gary Sullenger, PhD, United Education Institute of San Diego	Chet Lathrop
James "Buddy" Thomas, Superior Planning, Inc.	Ailene McManus
William Trumpfheller, Nuffer, Smith, Tucker, Inc.	Joe Horiye
Frank Urtasun, SDG&E	Barry Lorge
Mike West, Fox Asset Management	Hal Gardner
Colin Wied, C. W. Wied Professional Corporation	Rudi Brewster
C. Michael Wright, MD, The Lifescore Clinic	unknown

Rotarians of the Quarter

Barry Lorge

Peter Bowie

Peter Duncan

Jeremiah Doran

Also in July, Philippe Lamoise, member of the Torrey Pines Rotary Club, was named "Honorary Rotarian of the Quarter" for all of his web work and assisting with roasts.

▲ *President Jim Hughes presents a Rotarian of the Quarter award to Barry Lorge.*

▲ *President Jim Hughes presents an Honorary Rotarian of the Quarter award to Philippe Lamoise.*

Board of Directors, 2005–2006

James M. Hughes, President

Daryl E. "Debbie" Day, President-elect

Barbara "Bink" Cook, Secretary

Suzanne "Suzy" Spafford, Treasurer

Thomas R. Vecchione, MD, Past President

Robert C. Fletcher

Wayne K. Goodermote

Richard M. Green, DPM

Albert T. Harutunian III

Robert G. Russell, Jr.

Bonnie Schwartz

Nancy Scott

Richard A. Troncone

Diana D. Venable

Geri Warnke

In Memoriam

Arthur L. Austin

Harney M. Cordua, MD

Philip E. Del Campo

Pauline des Granges

Ferdinand Fletcher (Past President)

Hal Gardner

Charles G. Kerch

Estelle Kassebaum

Lieutenant General Lou Metzger, USMC (Ret.)

Homer D. Peabody, Jr., MD (Past President)

Haddon Peck, MD

Rear Admiral Herbert G. Stoecklein

Diana D. Venable

———————

Grotarian Events

Grotarians enjoyed several special events, including two evening sails on America's Cup boats. The San Diego collection of classic cars, the Ruben H. Fleet Space Theater, and San Diego's Historic Wind Tunnel events were all crowd pleasers. *The Constant Wife* at the Globe Theater was enjoyed by all who attended.

———————

Foreign/Exotic Make-ups

Rotarians do get around. Make-ups were reported by Paul Hartley, Jr., Vienna-West, Austria; Bink Cook, Samford Valley, Australia; Dick Sullivan, Paris, France; Linda Stirling, Geneva, Switzerland; Betty Hubbard, Interlaken, Switzerland; Jim Groen, Mukono, Uganda; Barbara Bry, Kowloon, Hong Kong; Joe Farrage, Rotary Club of Monaco; Jo Dee Jacob, Moruya, Australia; Linda Stirling, Rotary Club of Panama, Nordeste; and Cathryn Campbell, Kowloon, Hong Kong. While volunteering for MOST, Doug Arbon, Gene Rumsey, Jr., Bill Ward, and Tom Vecchione visited the Rotary Club of Tula, Hidalgo, Mexico.

The cruising Rotarians included Nikki and Ben Clay on the *Seven Seas Voyager* and Wayne Goodermote aboard a Viking River Cruise. Others were Bill Herrin, *Harmony G.*; Joan Friedenberg, *Mercury*; Natasha Josefowitz and Herman Gadon, *Queen Mary 2*; Ken Andersen, *Mercy*; Don Spanninga, *Galaxy*; Bill Dick, MS *Amsterdam*; and Tom Gable, MS *Paul Gauguin*, Tahiti.

———————

◢ President Hughes' aunt, Barbara Cunningham, attended a meeting.

◢ Even Elvis (a.k.a. Steve Hubbard) paid a visit.

and inspired all with his thoughts on success. Even "Elvis" dropped by for a visit.

President Hughes welcomed his aunt, Barbara Cunningham, at a meeting.

May 11th was the first-ever joint meeting of Club 33, the City Club, and the San Diego County Bar Association. Speaker of the Day was FBI Director Robert Mueller, and local law enforcement was well represented. Retired police chief and new Mayor Jerry Sanders presented the key to the city to Mueller, who answered questions following his remarks. Hughes invoked his presidential prerogative and asked the final question: "Will we ever find out who killed JFK?" Mueller's response was swift and beautifully mastered—a handful of words that had no meaning whatsoever.

Casting sights further afield, Rotarians were informed and educated by Midge Costanza, formerly of the Carter White House, now of San Diego; Todd Buchholz, the former director of White House economic policy; and Tom Hall, assistant secretary of defense. Tom

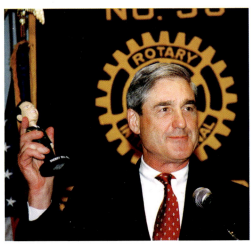

◢ FBI Director Robert Mueller.

Fox, the founder and CEO of New York Water Taxi, spoke about city greening, and Rotarians met Kyoto Laureate Professor Simon Levin from the Center for Biocomplexity at Princeton University. Dr. Peter Antoniou of CSU San Marcos presented "China: Friend or Foe." Dan Goldin, formerly with NASA, now chairman and CEO of the Intellisis Companies, described the Big Bang Theory, outer space, the formation of gaseous clouds, super hot matter, stars, and the ongoing "search for life" somewhere out there.

A lively debate was held in May on both sides of the illegal immigration issue.

Ruben Navarette of the *Union Tribune* and Peter Nunez, former U.S. attorney and former assistant secretary of the U.S. Treasury Department, discussed the pros and cons of policies surrounding the issue.

Sports

Thanks to Barry Lorge, sports-themed programs are always a big draw, and this year, Rotarians welcomed Pam Shriver (tennis), Vijay Amritraj (tennis), and Tom Wilson (Buick Open). Club 33's own Barry Lorge entertained the audience with his memories of covering Wimbledon.

Research and Educational Institutions

Local research and educational institutions provided much for members to think about, including the Research Ethics Program at UCSD; the California Condor Program at CRES at the San Diego Zoological Society, and the Scripps Institution of Oceanography.

Health issues were discussed by a variety of speakers, including Chris Van Gorder from Scripps Health, who brought a sobering post-Katrina message; Pat Kelly, the president of Pfizer, U.S.; Ginger Graham, the CEO of Amylin Pharmaceuticals; and world-famous Dr. Henry Heimlich (of the maneuver). Bringing all this closer to home, Rotarians were riveted by KGTV anchor Bill Griffith's gripping story of his personal experience with male breast cancer.

◂ President Hughes, Ruben Navarette, Gloria Penner, and Peter Nunez at the KPBS Editors Roundtable.

◢ Past presidents at Jim's roast.

◢ Peter Duncan, Steve Hubbard, and Jim Hughes at his roast.

◢ Back: Philippe Lamoise; front (from left): Barry Lorge, Debbie Day, and Stan Hartman at Jim's roast.

▲ *President Hughes with RI President Frank Devlyn (2001–2002).*

Economic Forecast

President Hughes was proud that Linda Stirling joined Bill Holland for the club's annual Economic Forecast. Special thanks and recognition went to past president Bert Wahlen for this signature program. Year-end predictions for the Dow Jones Industrial Average were Holland: 13,000, and Stirling: 11,778. The Dow Jones closed on December 29, 2006, at 12,463.

Mr. San Diego: Jerry Coleman, September 15, 2005

Reminding the audience of all that Padres announcer Jerry Coleman has accomplished, former mayor Dick Murphy spoke of Jerry's recent Ford C. Frick Award at the Baseball Hall of Fame in Cooperstown; on July 29, Coleman was inducted into the Marine Corps Sports Hall of Fame in Quantico, Virginia. Coleman reminisced about how lucky he felt when he arrived in San Diego in 1944. It looked good to a nineteen-year-old boy and he was smart enough to make it his permanent home. The rousing ovation that greeted Coleman showed him how lucky San Diegans felt that he came here all those years ago!

Fleet Week, October 13

Sandy Purdon, the chair of the Fleet Week luncheon, welcomed the Rotarians, the enlisted guests, and the "Music Machine," forty singers from Bonita High School who entertained with an abundance of energy and talent. Ty Nelson closed with "Proud to Be an American." Just before President Hughes excused the crowd to get a head start on the exodus out of the parking lot, red, white, and blue confetti and streamers were released from the ceiling—an impressive and very grand finale! Thanks to Paul Nestor for this pop! Unfortunately, after that, the Sheraton began charging $250 to clean up the confetti.

Salute to Local Heroes, January 12

The Salute to Local Heroes is one of the annual programs of Club 33 along with Mr./Ms. San Diego, Copley Scouting Awards, and others to recognize special people in the community. This year, chaired by Bob Arnhym, Sheriff Bill Kolender introduced Dawn Smith and Mitchell Caughron. District Attorney Bonnie Dumanis congratulated Carrie Quinn and Robert Gavina, and Police Chief Bill Landsdowne spoke of Michael Elkins and Anthony Lyon. Two additional awards were presented by President Jim Hughes to The San Diego Police Foundation and the Honorary Sheriff's Association.

◤ From left: President Jim, Bill Dick, and Jean Young.

▲ Steve Hubbard conducts the Rotary Chorus at the annual Holiday Luncheon.

▲ Jay and Carol Arnett and Laura and John Alito were greeted by Jean Young and Diana Venable at the annual Sweethearts Day luncheon.

▲ Top left: Bill Boyd, New Zealand, past president of Rotary International, and President Hughes.

▲ Top right: President Hughes and a guest speaker.

▲ Left: Geri Warnke greeted Steven Libman, managing director of the La Jolla Playhouse and a former member of Club 33.

▲ Above: Vice Admiral Jim Zortman, Naval Aviation, and Mike Morton at the Fleet Week luncheon.

THE ROAST

The Name is Bond… James Bond

Past president Tom Vecchione had his hands full as the past presidents escorted President Jim Hughes into the Westin Hotel Ballroom. Admonished to "remain in order," the audience quickly learned that Jim fancied himself the successor in a long line of actors who portrayed James Bond. Film clips verified his attempts to copycat Agent 007, although he expressed a preference for 033 as his favorite number. In spite of some evidence of possible looting of the Rotary treasury, he managed to hoodwink both RI President Frank Devlyn and FBI Chief Robert Mueller. After all, Jim's father was an FBI agent!

Turning his attention to filmmaking and aviation, film clips showed Howard Hughes taking on the film censorship board, escorting starlets down the red carpet, and narrowly escaping a Senate hearing. With the Club 33 Singers, musical numbers went from one extreme to another with selections from *You're a Good Man, Charlie Brown*, with solos by Suzy Spafford and Peter Duncan, and *Dirty Rotten Scoundrels* by Steve Hubbard and Peter Duncan. A heartfelt tribute by Paul Hartley, Jr. (Jim's second cousin) closed the ceremony. But, all good things have to come to an end and Jim got the end of the Barry Lorge (creator) and Philippe Lamoise (animator) Demotions. It was the final curtain for all three, being the last time Lorge and Lamoise produced a roast.

Jim later shared that early in his term, a prominent, active member of Club 33 stated to him, "I don't know why anyone would want to be president of San Diego Rotary; it's the worst job." Jim replied, "You've got it all wrong. Being president of this club is a great honor and is the best job in the club." Jim has said that his term in office was one of the best experiences of his life.

▲ Above: Rotary International past president Cliff Dochterman threw out the first pitch in the Rotary Flag Court dedication game at Petco Park.

◤ Left: Workers place the Rotary Wheel in the Rotary Flag Court at Petco Park.

CHAPTER SIX

Daryl E. "Debbie" Day

2006–2007

> *Never in my wildest dreams did I ever consider*
> *I would be president of Club 33.*
> *What a thrill! What an honor!*

▲ CHANGE OF COMMAND

D-Day at the Rotary

On July 6, 2006, Daryl E. "Debbie" Day took the helm of Club 33, donned the president's pin, wielded the gavel, and gave Rotarians a peek into the year to come. Amid a sea of "Debbie's Fan Club" signs, she announced that her three major goals would be continuing the search for a community project, finalizing the technology initiative, and continuing membership attraction and retention.

She also told the group that her speaker's gifts each week would be books to help populate the School in the Park Program at Hamilton Elementary School. Each speaker would be given a copy of *Challenging the Classroom Standard Through Museum-based Education* to keep. After swearing in the new president, Mayor Jerry Sanders signed the first book on snakes and reptiles.

Fining continued to play a big role. During her second meeting, President Day fined fifty-eight-year member Norm Roberts for placing San Diego Natural History Museum fliers on all the tables. Roberts shared news of the Dead Sea Scrolls exhibition set to open in June 2007. He offered to pay a ten-dollar fine; Day said, "OK, but ten dollars for each year of membership!" Imagine what the authors of those scrolls would have paid.

Later on, Hugh Carter was dinged for his fifty years in Club 33, which added up to $5,000, and past president Jim Hughes happily paid $1,500 for his fifteen years of perfect attendance.

▴ Mayor Jerry Sanders and President Debbie Day.

▴ Speaker Michael Hagar of the San Diego Natural History Museum and President Day.

SERVICE ABOVE SELF

In a September 15th email to members, Day announced that the twenty proposed community projects designed to celebrate the Rotary Club 33 Centennial in a BIG way had been narrowed down to three: Rotary Village Center, part of Enterprise Village, where students learn enterprise and manage businesses; Rotary/UCSD Mobile Health Clinic; and San Diego Rotary Centennial Education Center, a collaborative project between Club 33, the NTC Foundation, and the U.S. Navy. In December, Day told the membership that while all the projects received strong votes, no one project received overwhelming support. The projects would continue to be examined and reviewed and would be on track to begin in 2008 and completed by the Centennial Celebration in 2011.

September brought the annual Rotary fishing trip, chaired for the past fourteen years by Bob Fletcher, who caught a 110-pound yellowfin tuna! The annual "Big Fish" award was won by G. T. Frost. In December, Jo Dee Jacob chaired the annual auction supporting

scholarships which had been renamed the Diana Venable Scholarship Fund, honoring the late Diana Venable, who passed away in June 2006. The auction raised over $41,000. The second annual Rotarians at Work Day in April was chaired by Joe Mannino and ably assisted by eleven project managers. In May, Club 33 heard an update about the last two MOST trips to Mexico.

Monarch High School student Jessica Captain reported at the June 14 meeting on her trip of a lifetime to Antarctica. Also assisted by funding from the Robert Swan Foundation, the trip included a stay at E Base, where the group cleaned up after past expeditions, played cricket on an ice cap, and worked on scientific experiments. What an experience!

Club 33 Members are Honored

Several service awards from other organizations were presented to members of Club 33, including Frank Arrington, who was named "Fundraiser of the Year" at the annual National Philanthropy Day luncheon in November, and Dr. Thomas Vecchione, who received the Poverello Medal from Franciscan University

▲ Jo Dee Jacob and
Cliff Dochterman.

supporting the Rotary Youth Exchange, which took place from November through January.

Fary Moini and Steve Brown, members of the Golden Triangle Rotary Club, presented a fascinating program regarding the opportunity to mentor the Rotary Club of Kabul. Although travel to Afghanistan was not required, the two reported that during the eleven trips made there over the last four years, they had not encountered any problems.

in Steubenville, Ohio. Joe Craver and Jo Dee Jacob were recipients of The Cliff Dochterman Award, Rotary International's Community Service Award. The San Diego Art Institute presented their prestigious Ginger Award to Joyce Gattas. This award honors an individual or organization for exceptional efforts in the visual arts in Southern California. Darlene Davies received a Millennium Award from Friends of Balboa Park. In addition, November 14, 2006 was declared "Darlene Davies Day" by both the city and county of San Diego. She was honored for a long and valued record of community service in a resolution introduced by Senator Christine Kehoe.

Youth-oriented service projects included hosting visiting high school students at meetings, reading at various San Diego area schools, and

MEMBERSHIP

Fellowship, Camaraderie, and Engagement

Fun Events

Rotarians enjoyed two summer nights with the Padres at Petco Park, and the annual Sail

Camp Enterprise, April 12

Chaired by Bonnie Schwartz, the Camp Enterprise luncheon featured Brian Lange, who used music to bridge the intergenerational gap. Brian's hip-hop conversation with his dad and fellow Rotarian Roy Lange was fun for all and a great introduction for the students embarking on their Camp Enterprise weekend.

▲ Jill Spitzer and Debbie Day welcomed Camp Enterprise participants.

▲ The Doctors Rumsey: Gene, Jr., and Gene, Sr.

▲ Guy Maddox and Mike Morton enjoyed the Rotary Sail and BBQ.

▲ Bob Myers (right) prepared to cut off Chris Cramer's Cloud 9 Shuttle tie. With them is Cloud 9 founder John Hawkins.

and BBQ was held at the end of September. The first leg of the interclub golf tourney was held on October 13, when winners of the first leg were—gasp!—Bonnie Schwartz and Bob Mattis.

Additional opportunities for fellowship included The Paul Harris Dinner Dance in November and the March club tennis tournament, which was won—again—by Vern Aguirre.

Happy Significant Birthday to Bob Cleator, Sr., on his ninetieth!

Club 33 Members Make the News

Reint Reinders retired as president of the Convention and Visitors Bureau. Robert Horsman was named the new president of the San Diego Chamber of Commerce. *Barron*'s ranked Linda Stirling as twenty-eighth in the nation on their list of "Top Women Money Managers."

Health-related News

Due to health reasons, Barry Lorge resigned as president-elect. Club 33 sent very good wishes to Barry Lorge for his recovery. On August 31, Geri Warnke was named president-elect. In May, Mike Caruso shared news that he received a brand-new heart. After appropriate recovery time, he was "good as new!"

PROGRAMS

Continuing in strong Rotary tradition, many programs focused on the present and the future of the San Diego region. Rotarians welcomed updates from George Chamberlin regarding the San Diego economy and Joe Craver from the San Diego Regional Airport Authority (Where will that new airport go?). Representatives from the CCDC and Manchester Development Corporation brought information regarding revitalizing the

91

Grotarian Events

On August 15, Grotarians watched the Padres game from the lofty Diamond View Tower at Petco Park. In spite of a 3-2 loss to the Giants, it was a nice evening of fellowship and hot dogs! In October, a "behind the scenes" tour was held at the airport. March offered up a wonderful event at the Zoo, and the final Grotarian event of the year was at the National Fusion Facility on the campus of General Atomic.

Special "Tomato" Party for Paul Hartley, Jr.

▲ At Paul Hartley's "Tomato" Party.

▲ Card with sentiments from Hartley's "tomatoes."

▲ Paul Hartley, Jr. surrounded by his "tomatoes" (from left): Joanne Pastula, Patti Roscoe, Diane Bell, and Katherine Kennedy.

▲ Debbie Day and honoree Paul Hartley, Jr.

▲ Paul Hartley, Jr. serenaded his favorite "tomato," Charlotte.

Rotarians of the Quarter

Steve Mueller

Jo Dee C. Jacob

Sandy Mayberry

Bill Herrin

In Memoriam

Melvin M. Bartell

Joseph E. Jessop

Ronald H. Kendrick

R. Merl Ledford, MD

John A. Petersen

Eugene W. Rumsey, Sr., MD

Tom Sefton

Richard L. Sturgeon

Emory L. Thompson

William T. Ward

New Members

NAME	PRIMARY SPONSOR
Scott Bedingfield, Cavignac & Associates	Bob Russell
Kristin Bertell, Salk Institute for Biological Studies	John Hawkins
Merle Brodie, Alzheimer's Association	Leane Marchese
Mark Burgess, SanDiego.com, Inc.	Pat Goddard, Jr.
Reid Carr, Red Door Interactive	Kobe Bogaert
Derrick Cartwright, PhD, San Diego Museum of Art	Chuck Hellerich
Stephen Cushman, Automotive Dealer (Ret.)	Ben Clay
Andy Fichthorn, SeaWorld	George Gildred
Brad Gessner, San Diego Convention Center Corporation	Carol Wallace
Edward Gill, San Diego Symphony	Ben Clay
Ian Gill, Highland Partnership, Inc.	Doug Paul
Murray Goldman, PhD, Microprocessors (Ret.)	Paul J. Hartley, Jr.
Maureen Gray, KBM Building Services	Patti Roscoe
Walter Heiberg, The Corky McMillin Companies	Dick Troncone
Larry Hoeksema, Mosher, Drew, Watson & Ferguson	Jack Carpenter
Gayle Hom, New Americans Immigration Museum & Learning Center	Will Newbern
John Jedynak, The Window Factory, Inc.	Sheryl Bilbrey

(continued on next page)

(continued from previous page)

NAME	PRIMARY SPONSOR
Colette Jelineo, Cox Communications	Dick Troncone
Jennifer Kammerer, Law Offices of Jennifer Kammerer	John Hawkins
James Kidrick, San Diego Air & Space Museum	Mort Jorgensen
David Lang, Balboa Park Cultural Partnership	Bob Witty
Neil Larson, Mosher, Drew, Watson & Ferguson	Jack Carpenter
Kevin Leap, San Diego International Auto Show	Barbara Bry
John "Woody" Ledford, John W. Ledford, CPA	Richard Ledford
Susan Maddox, Sharp Healthcare	Pat Crowell
Keith McKenzie, Bernstein	Jack Berkman
Emile Misiraca, Independence Realty	Cindy Trowbridge
Rodney Moll, Trend Source	Dan Yates
David Oates, Stalwart Communications	Bob Russell
R. Kirk O'Brien, Aedifice Ideas	Paul Hartley III
David Peckinpaugh, San Diego Convention & Visitors Bureau	Lorin Stewart
Budd Rubin, DDS, MS, R. Rubin Dental Corporation	Frank Pavel, Jr.
Paige Ryan, ESOP Services, Inc.	Dan Yates
John Scarborough, Melhorn Construction, Inc.	Dan Yates
Ken Slaght, General Dynamics	Tom Gehring
Don Starkey, Comerica	Joanne Pastula
Larry Stirling, Superior Court (Ret.)	Linda Stirling
Judy Thompson, Judy Thompson & Associates	Richard Walker
Kevin Ward, Ward & Associates	Don Tartre
Allan Wasserman, Stewart Title Guaranty	David Porter
Jeff Wiemann, American Red Cross, San Diego/Imperial Counties	Richard Ledford

Foreign/Exotic Make-ups

Traveling Rotarians were at it again and made up meetings in a variety of foreign cities and ports. This year's travelers included Richard Coutts, Kowloon, Hong Kong; Paul Woo, Marina City, Singapore; Bink Cook, Herlev Rotary Club, Copenhagen; Lucy Killea, Colima, Mexico; Bill McColl, Whistler Millennium, British Columbia, Canada; Debbie Day, San Felipe, Baja California; Dick Jackson, San Felipe, Baja California; Bill McColl, St. John, Virgin Islands; Frank Arrington, Addis Ababa, Ethiopia; Bink Cook, Bulli, New South Wales, Australia; Jo Dee Jacob, Guam; Gary Gould, Schleswig/Gottorf Club, Germany; John Sands, Kisumu, Kenya; Judy Thompson, Kisumu, Kenya; Bob Kyle, Schleswig/Gottorf Club, Germany; and Jim M. Hughes, who visited multiple clubs in Uganda and Kenya.

The cruising Rotarians included Kenny Jones, *Star Princess*; Bill Herrin, *Statendam*; Kevin Enright, MS *Paul Gauguin*, Tahiti; Jay Goodwin, Norwegian Cruise Line; Joan Friedenberg, *Millennium*; Don Spanninga, *Splendor of the Seas*; Lewis Linson, *Zaandam*; Wayne Goodermote, MSY *Winstar*; Al Harutunian, *Ryndam*; and Ann Bethel, *Oosterdam*.

waterfront. Also, Martha Dennis, president of Commnexus, and Scott Silverman, from Second Chance/Strive, made informative presentations about their activities in the region.

Perennial program favorites included Michael Hagar, the Museum of Natural History; Ian Campbell, San Diego Opera; Des McAnuff, La Jolla Playhouse; and the San Diego Zoological Society. Lou Spisto, from the Old Globe Theater, brought special guest Hershey Felder, who appeared in the production of *George Gershwin Alone*. What a treat!

Two internationally known guests made appearances. Daniel Yankelovich, named by PR Week as one of the ten most influential people of the past century in the arena of public affairs, communications, and public relations, came in October. On December 7, Club 33 welcomed longtime PBS anchor Jim Lehrer, also the author of popular mysteries. Rotarians learned that Lehrer had served as a Marine with Club 33's own Bill Dick.

Health/Medical/Bio/Tech Programs

San Diego has long been recognized as the wireless and biotech capital of the world, and Club 33 heard about amazing future trends from Larry Smarr, director of the California Institute for Telecommunications and Information Technology (a partnership

▲ President Day and guest Peter Yarrow (of Peter, Paul and Mary).

95

between UC Irvine and UCSD) and Harry Gruber, UCSD professor of computer science and engineering, regarding what living in the future may be like. Also, Robert Hecht-Nielsen, a neuro network pioneer, summarized the Confabulation Theory, a concept not without controversy. Hecht-Nielsen explained the concept of San Diego as the birthplace, and ultimate world-dominant center, of confabulation technology that by 2020 could employ tens of millions of people.

San Diego is known as one of the healthiest places to live, and Club 33 welcomed updates from Dr. Richard Murphy, president/CEO, the Salk Institute; Gresham Bayne, MD, Call Doctor Medical Group; Katherine Sellick, CEO, Children's Hospital; Tommy Thompson, former U.S. secretary of the Department of Health and Human Services; Dr. Mimi Guarneri, Scripps Center for Integrative Medicine; and Bob Blancato, who spoke about "Aging Baby Boomers."

▲ Debbie Day, a special military guest, and Andy Hewitt.

Military

In addition to periodic updates from Club 33's Lieutenant Colonel Andy Hewitt,

▲ Club 33 Singers, front row (from left): Suzy Spafford, Kimberly Layton, Debbie Day, and Tess Nelson; back row: Peter Duncan, Larry Showley, Greg Zinser, George Harris, and Jack Anthony.

USMC, Rotarians were enlightened by Major General Sam Helland, USMC regarding the global War on Terror.

Education

San Diego is home to myriad educational institutions. On March 22, a panel moderated by Gloria Penner was held with SDSU President Stephen Weber and UCSD Chancellor Marye Anne Fox. In addition to providing much food for thought, Dr. Fox stated that by 2010, over 90 percent of PhDs in science will be awarded in Asia. The program was later broadcast on KPBS. In March, Rotarians welcomed Kyoto Laureate Issey Miyake, a world-renowned designer, and futurist David Brin, who brought a riveting "Look into Tomorrow's World."

In June, Rotarians listened to a fascinating presentation by UCSD professor Maurizio Seracini, who came to San Diego as a young man with the help of a Rotary fellowship. He now serves as director of the Center for Interdisciplinary Science for Art, Architecture and Archeology at UCSD. A current project is the search for DaVinci's "Battle of Anghian," a fresco lost for over 500 years. It is speculated to be buried behind a masterpiece painted on a plaster wall. Stay tuned….

Mr. San Diego: Paul Hartley, Jr., August 3

Mayor Jerry Sanders introduced Rotary past president Hartley as "a man of character, and a character." He pointed out that Hartley holds the record for the highest number of new members sponsored into Rotary and highlighted the myriad service and charitable organizations Hartley has served with seemingly limitless energy in the thirty-plus years since his retirement. Hartley listed four of his favorite volunteer commitments: The Armed Services YMCA, The Episcopal Church, Hoover High School (his alma mater), and Rotary Club 33. He closed by playing an enthusiastic rendition of "I've Been Working on the Railroad" on his famous ukulele. The audience joined in.

▲ Top: *President Day with Jerry Sanders and Paul Hartley, Jr. (Mr. San Diego).*

▲ Middle: *Doug Williams, Paul Hartley, Jr., and George McKinney.*

▲ Bottom: *Mayor Jerry Sanders, Paul Hartley, Jr. (Mr. San Diego), Ronne Froman, Kevin Faulconer, and Debbie Day.*

Fleet Week, October 5

The chair of Fleet Week 2006 was Lisa Richards and the luncheon chair was Andy Hewitt. The audience enjoyed guest speaker Chuck Long, head football coach at SDSU, who entertained with stories of his time in the NFL and the ingredients necessary to build a winning team.

▲ *General Paxton, Debbie Day, and a guest.*

Economic Forecast, January

The annual Economic Forecast luncheon featured Bill Holland and Linda Stirling. Their annual predictions were Holland: 14,000, and Stirling, 14,200. The Dow Jones Industrial Average closed on December 31, 2007, at 13,265.

Salute to Local Heroes, January 11

SDPD Chief Bill Landsdowne, Sheriff Bill Kolender, and County DA Bonnie Dumanis presented the 2007 honorees. Jason Bemis, Paula Stead, and Jenny Pino were honored for intervening to help save victims being beaten and stabbed. John Fontanini and Charles Moore helped bring robbers to justice. Angel Rivera saw what happened to a young rape victim, helped identify the assailant, and testified against him.

President Day presented a final award to the SDPD Crisis Intervention Team, a group of eighty-plus volunteers who have been the city's "emotional paramedics" since 1989.

▲ *President Day (back row, far left) stands with (back row, from third from left) Bonnie Dumanis, Bill Kolender, and Bill Landsdowne with award recipients at the Salute to Local Heroes.*

▲ *Buddy Thomas, President Day, Cliff Dochterman, and Executive Director Chet Lathrop.*

THE ROAST

The Life of Debbie Day

A musically themed program harkened back to President Day's student days at SDSU, where she was reported to have majored in "song, dance, and young men!" Musical treats accompanied a slideshow about various stages in Day's life including her christening as Daryl Elizabeth Day; the "adoption" of her nickname, "Debbie," when she was in the fifth grade; her post-college years; and life as a young mom in a Frank Hope, Sr.-designed home in Point Loma. Songstress Kimberly Layton sang "Que Sera, Sera" and the Club 33 Singers sang "It Had to Be You." Among the singers was former San Diego Rotarian Sandra Pay, who returned to surprise her close friend Debbie. It was revealed that after spending a few years working for various organizations, Debbie became the executive director of the Engineering and General Contractors Association—a 100-percent male organization. She joined Rotary in 1993 and followed Penny Allen and Patti Roscoe as Club 33's third woman president.

The Roast concluded with the presentation of the past president's pin, a third Paul Harris fellowship, and the final song, "We'll Be Seeing You." Debbie's Day was done!

▲ President Debbie Day with members of the Jacobs International Teen Leadership Institute sponsored by Gary and Jerri-Ann Jacobs.

▲ President Debbie Day kicks off the annual holiday program with the Rotary Chorus.

CHAPTER SEVEN

Geri Ann Warnke

2007–2008

" Get Ready, Get Set, Get Moving! "

■ **TWO DECADES AFTER SHE JOINED ROTARY, GERI ANN WARNKE SAW PERHAPS MORE** changes and transitions in the club than anyone could recall in recent memory. From changes in the way members communicated to a transformation of office space to a new executive director, things in Club 33 were definitely on a new trajectory!

CHANGE OF COMMAND

The Change of Command ceremony on July 5 began with a pair of poems by Natasha Josefowitz, one of the first women members of Club 33. Almost-president Geri Warnke, also one of the first women to join, noted that this was her twentieth year as a Rotarian.

Speaker Pat Crowell told the story of how women were welcomed into Rotary after a Supreme Court ruling upheld a lawsuit filed by the Los Angeles (Duarte) Chapter. Warnke announced big plans, including an emphasis on health, and she broached the subject of

skipping dessert once a month. Dessert-skipping brought a very mixed response, but to offset those dessert calories, she gifted each member of Club 33 with their very own pedometer—Warnke was ready to move!

Determined that she would never again hear a cell phone ring during a guest speaker's presentation, Warnke banned cell phones during meetings—forever! She instituted a $500 fine, but apparently John Hawkins missed the memo; he was the first to pay up! It turned out to be an effective and oh-so-lucrative way to reinforce good manners.

A Year of Firsts

In July, Chet Lathrop announced that, after eighteen years as the executive director of Club 33, he would be retiring. This prompted a search for a new executive director under the leadership of co-chairs Mary Colacicco and Vincent Mudd. Bente Hansen & Associates, executive search firm, gave valuable direction. Ultimately, over one hundred applications were received and a new executive director, Bruce Hunt, was hired in January 2008. February 7 would be declared "Chet Lathrop Day" in honor of his dedication and service to the club for so many years.

In October, devastating and far-reaching wildfires caused a rare cancellation of a Club 33 Thursday meeting. Fortunately, the website enabled members to stay in touch with each other and locate those needing assistance during the disaster.

A major project was the complete reorganization of the club's financial policies, procedures, and reporting, including the first audit. The establishment of a

▲ President Geri Warnke welcomed her parents, Gerald and Jeanne Warnke, at her installation.

▲ Club 33 Walkers.

▲ Middle left: Mayor Jerry Sanders congratulated President Geri Ann Warnke at her installation.

▲ Middle: President Warnke (left) and Natasha Josefowitz at the installation.

▲ Above: Close friends helped President Warnke celebrate her installation.

Finance Committee was critical and occurred under the watchful eyes of Woody Ledford, Bruce Blakley, and Ed Kitrosser. Later in the year, Warnke honored them as "Rotarians of the Quarter" for the fourth quarter. Another first was the May 1st meeting, which was completely devoted to club business. Attendees were encouraged to ask questions and learn more "insider information." At the same time, Hal Sadler was named chair of the task force to find a permanent location for the club. In addition, it was decided to look carefully at the by-laws, which hadn't been changed since 1911. Tyler Cramer, Al Harutunian, and Bob Russell stepped up for this task.

November brought the first Legacy Luncheon to honor Rotarians who had been members for forty years or more. Chaired by Peg Eddy, the luncheon featured a twenty-two-minute video produced by Warnke. In it, she interviewed more than a dozen Rotarian emeriti who shared their stories and memories of club activities.

Refurbishment of the club's physical space began in the fall of 2007 with a move into storage space (really!). Many club members made sure that club business continued in spite of the disruption. Yeoman work by member Jean Young resulted in new colors and décor and a much-needed conference room shared with other building tenants. Thanks to the extraordinary efforts of Jerry Doran and Jim Hughes, technology updates and enhancements brought Club 33 even further into the twenty-first century! The *Rotator* was transformed and an overhaul of the entire website added an audio component and photo gallery. More use of email and online reservations resulted in lowered printing and mailing costs. Over time, Club 33 would be "going green!"

Peter Bowie took the Project Allocation Committee to a new level and gave structure and organization to the funding process.

Another Club 33 first was to change the invocation to the "Inspirational Moment" and ask newer club members—those who had joined in the preceding eighteen months—to deliver the weekly "moment." The Club 33 Donor Honor Roll first appeared in a June 2008 *Rotator*.

For many, Club 33 had become another full-time job, so each quarter, President Warnke opened her home to wine and dine the hardworking board members. She never let them forget how much she appreciated them!

SERVICE ABOVE SELF

In honor of Warnke's presidential year, non-Rotarians Nora and Alan Jaffee presented Club 33 with a $10,000 check. Warnke turned the check over to the Diana Venable Scholarship Fund. In another "first," the December 6th Diana Venable Auction proceeds were exclusively devoted to this fund. The entire meeting was devoted to the Auction Committee under the direction and leadership of Nancy Scott and Jo Dee Jacob and, as a result, over $60,000 was raised for scholarships.

World Community Service work days in Tecate were held in September, October, January, and February. Richard Jackson and Chris Sichel gave frequent updates to club members.

Amnon Ben-Yehuda and his "Don't Wait, Vaccinate" Committee were very busy at multiple clinics in San Diego.

MOST Celebrates its Twentieth Anniversary

The MOST team visited Ciudad Valles (300 miles northeast of Mexico City) in October and Tula, Mexico, in March. The November 8th meeting celebrated the twentieth anniversary of Rotary's involvement with MOST. Pat Robinson and Drs. Bill Davidson, Tom Vecchione, and Doug Arbon led the celebration. It was announced that over 7,000 free surgeries had been performed.

Currently, supplies are gathered at Mercy Hospital and flown into small Mexican villages. Volunteers include surgeons, anesthesiologists, and nurses. Ricardo Escandon, past president of the National City Club, has been the voice and face of MOST in Mexico for twenty-four years. He researches villages and works with local Rotary clubs to coordinate the program. On screening day, typically 500 people show up with a hope of getting surgery, but only 300 can be selected.

Vecchione's daughter, Gina, produced a touching video of MOST over the years, and on August 2, PBS aired the documentary *Miracles in Tula*.

Fish Across the Border, January 14

Under the leadership of Bob Fletcher, twenty-seven participants brought back 160 albacore from the fall club fishing trip. In January, many Rotarians from Southern California joined the Ensenada Rotary Club and filled 900 grocery bags of food for needy families in the greater Ensenada area. After a hard day of packing the bags, the Ensenada Club hosted a BBQ at the home of Dr. Eloy Perez. Excellent news was that the returning Rotarians only had an eighteen-minute wait at the border—a new record—and they were home in time to watch the Chargers beat the Titans!

Camp Enterprise Celebrates its Thirty-third Anniversary, April 26

Peter Duncan chaired Club 33's thirty-third anniversary of Camp Enterprise. Since its founding, 2,900 high school juniors have participated. This year, eighty-five students participated, and the speaker was Garry Ridge, president/CEO of WD-40, a homegrown $500-million company. The first Camp Enterprise chair was Chet Lathrop. Club 33's new "Chet Lathrop Trophy" was established to honor the recently retired executive director and presented to the team that best exemplified the four-way test in their business model presentations.

Rotarians at Work Day, April 26

Chaired by Lewis Linson, this year's locations included the Mission Valley Preserve Gardens, YAHO Storefront Kitchen, St. Paul Senior Homes, and Veterans Village.

MEMBERSHIP

Fellowship, Camaraderie, and Engagement

Nothing says FUN like Rotary! In spite of the hard work and change going on both in Rotary and in the lives of Club 33 members, people found time for fun and fellowship. The eighth annual Sail and BBQ was held on October 13 and was attended by ninety Rotarians and guests.

At a golf outing held on October 12, Dick Green led the pack with a low net of 70. Other scores were low gross: Tom Wilson (73) and Dick Green (81); low net: Larry Showley (71) joining Dick Green; and Marten Barry (73). Bonnie Schwartz led the women's division in all categories. Ultimately, the Jack Thompson Trophy was won by Murray Goldman.

Another enjoyable evening was the district Paul Harris Gala held at the Hilton San Diego Resort on November 17. The first Holiday Party in ten years was given by past presidents at the home of President Warnke and hubby, Joe Kennedy. In more athletic pursuits, Club 33 tennis players enjoyed sets at the Barnes Tennis Center, and a night out at Petco Park was enjoyed by athletes and non-athletes alike.

Emphasis on Health

In her plans for the year, Warnke placed an emphasis on health information in general and the health of Club 33 members in particular. Rotary Walks were held at Mission Bay Park in September, November, January, and May. A month-long pedometer contest was held in May to see who walked the most steps. In the over-forty age group, Dick Sullivan won with 437,208 steps (218 miles). Pauline Hill, Club 33's executive assistant, won the under-forty age group with 210,000 steps (104 miles). She credited her win as a result of running to keep up with Warnke and the board! Mike Morton generously donated dinner for two at Azul's in La Jolla.

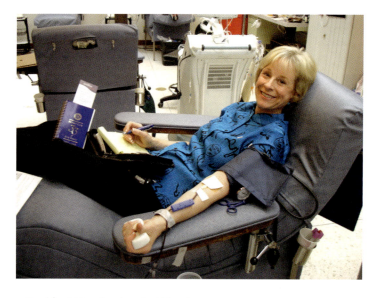

◢ President Warnke donated blood.

▲ Joining President Warnke in her birthday celebration were (from left) Stan Hartman, Dick Green, and Dick Troncone.

▲ Geri Warnke celebrated her birthday with (from left) her husband, Joe Kennedy, MD; her sister, Melinda Mical Claussen; and past president Patti Roscoe.

Many Good Deeds

Rotarians were honored by local organizations for a variety of good deeds. October 9th was declared "Michael Brunker Day" by the City of San Diego. Brunker was honored for his work as executive director of the Jackie Robinson YMCA. Geri Warnke received the Community Service Award from the "Women Who Mean Business"

awards. Reid Carr was named "Most Admired CEO in San Diego" by the *San Diego Business Journal*. Patti Roscoe and Brigadier General Angela Salinas were named two of the "10 Cool Women of 2008" by the Girl Scouts of San Diego. Suzy Spafford and Pat Caughey received the Cliff Dochterman Award for

▲ Shelly Brockett (center) celebrated his birthday with President Warnke and George Jessop.

Board of Directors, 2007–2008

Geri Warnke, President
Stanford F. Hartman, Jr., President-elect
Suzanne "Suzy" Spafford, Secretary/Treasurer
Daryl E. "Debbie" Day, Past President
Jack R. Anthony, OD
Barbara "Bink" Cook
Richard A. DeBolt
Peter L. Duncan

Andrew W. Hewitt
J. Stephen Hubbard
Barry S. Lorge*
Sandra L. Mayberry
Charles J. Pretto
Bonnie Schwartz
Richard A. Troncone

Mr. Lorge passed away on June 5, 2008, and Tyler Cramer stepped in.

outstanding Scouting Rotarians. Darlene Davies received a coveted Monty Award, SDSU's highest award for alumni achievement. In 2007, Davies completed two terms on the Balboa Park Committee, having served as both vice chair and chair.

Several members of Club 33 celebrated significant birthdays this year, including Bob Cleator, Sr. on June 19 (ninety-two), Shelly Brockett on September 11 (ninety-four), and Vaughn Lyons on October 18 (ninety).

Grotarian Events

Grotarians advanced their knowledge base of all things Rotary while enjoying a variety of events. A sail on *The America*, a tour of the Dead Sea Scrolls at the Natural History Museum, a fireside chat, and on-site events at the Sheriff's Crime Lab and Petco Park were special events enjoyed by all.

▲ Left: *Natasha Josefowitz and Herman Gadon.*

▲ Right: *Barry Lorge and President Warnke.*

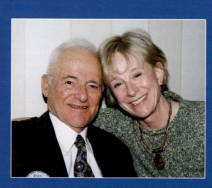

▲ *Paul Hartley, Jr. and President Warnke.*

▲ *From left: Jim Hughes, Debbie Day, Tom Vecchione, Paul Hartley, Jr., Bink Cook, and Charlotte Hartley gather around Barry Lorge (seated).*

Rotarians of the Quarter

Tom Gehring

Peg Eddy

Joe Horiye

Bruce Blakley

Ed Kitrosser

Woody Ledford

New Members

NAME	PRIMARY SPONSOR
Richard Andersen, San Diego Padres	Patti Roscoe
Robert W. Armstrong, San Diego Private Bank	G. T. Frost
Steve Bond, TAG	Tom Gable
Reo Carr, *San Diego Business Journal*	Susan Snow
Darren Cecil, Sandler Sales Institute	Neil Schneider
Joe Dolphin, Medevac, Inc. (Ret.)	Dennis Kenneally
Judy Forrester, LEAD San Diego	Joyce Glazer
Martin Goodman, Residential Capital	Dan Yates
Douglas Gordon, Douglas B. Gordon, PC	Stan Hartman
Nancy Graham, CCDC	Hal Sadler
Roger Haines, U.S. Attorney's Office	Colin Wied
Joy L. Hamer, RN, OCN, Sidney Kimmel Cancer Center	Paul J. Hartley, Jr.
Carlos Heredia, California Counsel Group, Inc.	Tyler Cramer
Bruce A. Hunt, Rotary Club of San Diego	Ben Clay
Darrah Johnson, Planned Parenthood of San Diego & Riverside Counties	Barbara Bry
Dennis M. Kenneally, Business Associates International, LLC	Jim Hall
Rick McElvain, Tax Projects Group	Craig Nelson
Michael Murphy, American Medical Response	Chris Sichel
David Oates, Stalwart Communications	Bob Russell
Patricia G. O'Connor, Fashion Careers College	Joyce Glazer
Jennifer Perkins, Eat Drink & Sleep	Richard Ledford
The Rev. Dr. John Powell, Point Loma Community Presbyterian Church	Suzy Spafford
Mari Lyn Salvador, San Diego Museum of Man	Marie Huff
Todd Struyk, Cal Pacific Mortgage Brokerage, AA	Paul Hartley III
Leroy Tomlinson, Engineering (Ret.)	Paul J. Hartley, Jr.
John Van Deusen, Financial Recruiting Solutions	Jeremiah Doran

In Memoriam

Gerald B. Allen

William G. Fiss

Henry Garnjobst, Jr.

James M. Lee (Former Club 33 Executive Director)

Barry S. Lorge

Joseph W. Telford, MD

PROGRAMS

Club 33 programs covered a wide range of topics from global issues to those in Rotarians' own backyards. With an emphasis on health, Rotarians heard from local healthcare centers and physicians with expertise in specific health concerns. A new program feature, Dr. Matt Hom's "Health Moment," was welcomed by members who were amazed at the amount of health news he could pack into ninety seconds.

Elizabeth Barrett-Connor, MD, chief of epidemiology at UCSD Medical Center, presented an informative program on osteoporosis. Gene Rumsey, Jr., MD addressed issues surrounding obesity. Warren Kessler, MD and Carol Salem, MD spoke about prostate cancer, and Rotarian Dick Green, DPM presented a program on healthy feet.

Chris Van Gorder, president and chief executive officer of Scripps Healthcare, described the selection of Scripps as one of the Fortune 500 "Best Companies to Work for in 2007." Van Gorder also was named to the "100 Most Powerful People in Healthcare" list. Dan Gross, executive vice president for hospital operations at Sharp Healthcare, told the story of Sharp, which began in 1955 and is now close to completing a magnificent new facility in Kearny Mesa.

Programs more global in nature included presentations by Joseph Nyumah Boakai, the vice president of Liberia; Robert Goff, an expert in India and Uganda; and Jose Miguel Isulza, the secretary general of the Organization of the Americas. In addition, Club 33 heard from Dr. Donald Manahan, USC Department of Biological Sciences, and Dr. Gladys Kalema-Zikusoka, founder and CEO of Conservation Through Public Health. San Diego County Supervisor Ron Roberts presented an extensive and fascinating slideshow on China.

Closer-to-home speakers included Alan Bersin, San Diego Airport; Ruben Barrales,

▲ From left: Richard Coutts, Geri Warnke, and Dr. Joseph Nyumah Boakai, vice president of Liberia.

San Diego Chamber of Commerce; Doug Sawyer, United Way; Sharon Lawrence, president, Voices for Children; and Rachel Teagle, executive director, Children's Museum of San Diego. In addition, Maureen Stapleton, San Diego County Water Authority, and Joe Grindstaff, State of California Resources Agency, updated Rotarians on the current water policies. David Wescoe talked about the San Diego City Employees Retirement System, and Doug Wilson presented a look back at twenty-five years of downtown history. In May, Gloria Penner, KPBS, moderated her program, Editors Roundtable, which brought together the *Union Tribune*, *San Diego Voice and Viewpoint*, and *San Diego Metropolitan Magazine*. It was later broadcast on KPBS.

Words and books made interesting program topics this year and included *BOOM!* author Jackie Freiberg; Susan Arnout Smith, author of *The Timer Game*; and Joseph Wambaugh, author of countless best-sellers. Dan Walters, *Sacramento Bee* columnist,

brought a pessimistic view of the state of our state. Richard Lederer from KPBS, Rotarians' favorite wordsmith, did not disappoint.

Educationally oriented programs included Judge James Milliken, who gave an update on the San Pasqual Academy. Dr. Tony Haymet, Scripps Institution of Oceanography, and Kati Haycock, president of the Educational Trust in Washington, D.C., were welcomed. In addition, Club 33 heard from Kyoto Lauretes Dr. Hiroo Kanamori and Pina Bausch.

Sports

Sports programs included San Diego's own Tony Gwynn, who spoke about his upcoming induction into the Baseball Hall of Fame, and before he could get a word out, the Club 33 Singers sang an electrifying version of "Take Me Out to the Ballgame!" Gwynn was obviously humbled at the Hall of Fame prospect and tried out a bit of his speech on the audience. Exemplifying Rotary's four-way

▲ Chemist Dr. Hiroo Inokuchi, eighty, professor emeritus of the University of Tokyo and the Institute for Molecular Science; geophysicist Dr. Hiroo Kanamori, seventy, professor emeritus of California Institute of Technology; Malin Burnham; choreographer and artistic director Pina Bausch, sixty-six; and Geri Warnke.

◢ From left: Executive Assistant Pauline Hill, President Warnke, Brigadier General Angie Salinas, and Bruce Binkowski.

◢ President Warnke introduced a friend and Rotary member from Spain, David De Vesa.

◢ President Warnke and George Gildred at the Sweethearts Day program.

test in so many ways, Gwynn was presented with a sapphire Paul Harris Fellow medal as Club 33's special thanks "for who you are and all you do."

The December Holiday Bowl program featured former NFL receiver Phil McConkey, who, in 1978, caught the winning touchdown for Navy in the first-ever Holiday Bowl. He shared wonderful memories of playing in the Holiday Bowl and visiting San Diego, which he now calls home.

THE ROAST

The Energizer Geri

Preceding her grand entrance, a six-piece marching band played "The Bunny Hop" as Geri "The Energizer Bunny" Warnke marched into the June 26th meeting wearing a fetching pink bunny suit complete with the requisite cottontail. The Club 33 Singers sang "Geri-fied" words to "Loco-Motion" and participants included Natasha Josefowitz, who read her original poem highlighting the year. Ben Clay presented a *This is Your Life* program including career shots of Geri as a private pilot, lion-tamer, and horsewoman.

In a more serious tone, Mark Trotter lauded the many impressive accomplishments of Geri's year including the Legacy Luncheon, the focus on health, the Club 33 reorganization,

Economic Forecast, January 3

Bill Holland and John Folsom (subbing for his business partner, Linda Stirling) presented the annual Economic Forecast. Holland said that 2007 had been a good year with record highs. Folsom spoke of sky-rocketing oil and gold prices. Don Bauder, now living in Colorado, was contacted by phone and predicted a 60-percent chance of recession in the U.S. in 2008 and an 80-percent chance in San Diego. Specific predictions were not recorded. The Dow Jones Industrial Average closed on December 31, 2008, at 8,776.

In January, past district governor Wayne Cusick, founder of the Paul Harris Society in 1997, was honored by Club 33 for "immense service" to Rotary International. Wilf Wilkinson, Rotary International president, was on hand to offer his congratulations as well.

District Governor Jim O'Meara paid his visit to Club 33 on October 4.

▲ Past district governor Wayne Cusick (left), Geri Warnke, and RI President Wilf Wilkinson.

and raising the "amazing sum of $283,000." In closing, Geri stated, "It brings me to tears to think of my outstanding and hardworking board. Thank you, thank you."

After receiving the traditional Club 33 gift box, Geri presented a gift of her own to the club, a brand-new custom-built podium to honor the members of her board, whom she described as "the heart and soul of a very special year."

▲ From left: George Gildred, Mort Jorgensen, Geri Warnke, Bill McDade, and Ross Pyle.

Past presidents with President Geri Warnke at her roast.

President Geri with Rotary "First Man" Joe Kennedy, MD.

President Geri with her gift box.

Mr. San Diego: Harold Sadler, August 23, 2007

The audience was reminded that the honor of the title Mr. or Ms. San Diego goes to a person who has contributed outstanding community betterment to the San Diego region in a variety of ways through his or her efforts over a long period of time. Harold Sadler was then introduced as the 2007 Mr. San Diego. After being thanked for his service, Sadler highlighted the roles played by many in the growth of San Diego. Asked whether the Chargers should stay or go, he responded, "Stay where they are." His response to a question regarding development on the waterfront was that a symbolic building, like the Sydney Opera House, is needed.

▲ Top: *Mr. San Diego Hal Sadler (left) and Mayor Jerry Sanders.*

▲ Left: *Past Mr. San Diego recipients (from left): Herb Klein, Bruce Moore, and Jim Mulvaney.*

Fleet Week, October 11

Fleet Week luncheon chair Andy Hewitt welcomed hundreds as they streamed into the white tent known as the Pavilion. The Navy Brass Combo set the tone with their spirited patriotic music. The speaker was double-amputee Sergeant First Class Dana Bowman, U.S. Army (Ret.), who lost both legs in a military skydiving accident. He imparted hope and dignity to those experiencing personal grief and despair. He was thanked by a rousing Rotary standing ovation, and the program closed with Steve Hubbard singing "America the Beautiful."

Salute to Local Heroes, January 10

At the Salute to Local Heroes, Police Chief Bill Landsdowne described the heroic acts by Joaquin Tena, who assisted a domestic violence victim, and Josefina and Bob Holper, who aided two sexual assault victims. DA Bonnie Dumanis told of the courage of Lorin Clark, who prevented an armed robbery, and Eddie Gregory, who was instrumental in the apprehension and arrest of a car-jacking suspect. Sheriff Bill Kolender introduced Ralph Bishop, Verlon Cox, and Clarence Good, who came to the aid of two young stabbing victims. The Rotary Club 33 Organization Award was presented to the San Diego Prevention Coalition and accepted by Board President Ron Sahmel. The program on crystal meth brought together many different agencies in San Diego County.

New Executive Director: Bruce A. Hunt

Bruce A. Hunt, a senior executive experienced in the leadership and management of non-profit, hospitality, finance, and education institutions, was selected as Club 33's executive director in January 2008. He was the front office manager at the Hotel del Coronado from 1995 to 1999 prior to moving to the Bay Area.

A certified financial planner and stockbroker, Hunt is a former member of the Rotary Club of South Oklahoma City. He also has worked as an elementary school principal, classroom teacher, and restaurant manager. Hunt is a member of the San Diego Chapter of the American Society for Training and Development, a member of the Board of Youth Tennis San Diego, a member of the Executive Committee of the San Diego Sigma Chi Alumni Chapter, and a volunteer for the United States Tennis Association, the national governing body of tennis. Hunt recently returned to San Diego after serving as the executive director of the United States Tennis Association Northern California Section in Alameda, California.

▲ *President Warnke welcomed Bruce Hunt, the new executive director, into the membership.*

Chet Lathrop Day

February 7th was declared by Mayor Jerry Sanders to be "Chet Lathrop Day." This weekly meeting was "all about Chet!" A succession of speakers lauded Lathrop's years as a Rotarian and his eighteen years as executive director. District Governor Jim O'Meara presented an award from Rotary International recognizing Lathrop as "A Guardian of Rotary." The hotel staff served up a surprise Baked Alaska to Lathrop's table. Bruce Moore, founder of Camp Enterprise, reflected on Lathrop's important role as the first chair of Camp Enterprise, and Mark Trotter revealed how much Lathrop has cared for those in the extended Rotary family. The Club 33 Singers sang customized words to "Route 66" and led two sing-alongs. Craig Evanco presented Lathrop with a handcrafted wooden box filled with gifts as a token of Club 33's appreciation. All in all, it was described as a fine run!

▲ President Warnke and Chet Lathrop at the Change of Command.

▲ Sharon and Chet Lathrop at his farewell luncheon.

Holiday Luncheon

▲ The Rotary Holiday Chorus.

CHAPTER EIGHT

Stanford F. Hartman, Jr.

2008–2009

> *Being president of Rotary was one of the greatest*
> *opportunities I have had to serve our community.*

▲ CHANGE OF COMMAND

One day before the Fourth of July, democracy reigned and Stan "The Man" took command! Mayor Jerry Sanders installed President Stanford F. Hartman, Jr. as the ninety-ninth president of Club 33. Immediate past president Geri Warnke led off with a heartfelt speech describing Hartman as a successful businessman, active Rotarian, and hardworking community leader.

Hartman shared his ambitious agenda for the upcoming year. Each member was asked to take on a project. "Join a committee," he said, "to have fun and to be inspired." Continued planning for the centennial in 2011, a continued search for a permanent home for Club 33, and emphasis on member development were key goals for the year. Hartman described his Presidential Project: a micro-credit project in Mexico called the Bank of Hope (Financiera de Esperanza) led by Kenny Jones and Bink Cook. During the year, each speaker received a certificate from Hartman symbolizing a donation made to the project in his or her name.

Early in the year, Geri Warnke good-naturedly challenged (and heckled!) Hartman's fining ability. In response, he fined her $500! There was no more questioning his fining prowess! Another early fine was levied against David Oates, making him the first Club 33 member to make his annual $250 donation.

SERVICE ABOVE SELF

The sixteenth annual Rotary fishing trip in September kicked off a year of service projects. In January, 901 sacks of groceries were packed up to go with the fish. Another great trip made up of fun, fishing, and fellowship benefited needy families in Ensenada.

In November, the MOST team went to Chiapas, Mexico, where over 350 patients experienced 240 life-transforming surgeries.

January 17th found Rotarians in Tecate, Mexico, doing a bang-up job sprucing up a school building. Attending with World Community Service Day committee leader Mike Kenny were Jim Groen, Paul Hartley III, John Reid, Norbert Sanders, Don Teemsma and his daughter, Mariah, and Jerry Van Ert. In addition, members of the Tecate Rotary Club added to the fun and productive day.

The annual Rotarians at Work Day on April 25th drew ninety-six Rotarians plus more than one hundred family members and friends who volunteered for a dozen projects all over San Diego.

The "Christmas You Missed" took place on June 25th. Most of the 120 families were from the 3rd Marine Air Wing at MCAS Miramar. In all, 450 participated in the annual summer event.

▲ World Community Service Day found (from left) Don Teemsa, Norbert Sanders, and Paul Hartley III hard at work in Tijuana with members of the local Rotary Club.

▲ Mayor Jerry Sanders (right) prepares the induction for Stan Hartman as past president Geri Warnke looks on.

MEMBERSHIP

Fellowship, Camaraderie, and Engagement

▲ Rotarians at Work Day.

Opportunities for fun and fellowship began in fine style at the annual Day at the Races in August. Better yet, Dick Green won thirty-seven dollars, which he kindly donated to PolioPlus! Club 33-ers enjoyed three nights at Petco Park in August, September, and May. It is safe to say that Rotarians had more fun than the team, as the Padres lost the first two games to the Cubs (8-5) and the Dodgers (7-2). However, the Padres won 2-1 against the Giants in May. Go Padres! David Oates threw out the first pitch and the Club 33 Singers sang "The Star-Spangled Banner."

In a bit of a turnaround, a Military Affairs presentation to Club 33 from our troops in Iraq was handled by Bob Russell with an assist by Steve Hubbard and Bill Van De Weghe to get all those care packages out to the brave soldiers.

Rotarians and guests enjoyed the annual Sail and BBQ at the San Diego Yacht Club in October, and in November, sixty hearty folks

Diana Venable Auction, December 11

To date, $185,000 was raised for the Diana Venable Scholarship Fund, of which Sandy Sophal was the first recipient, toward the ten-year goal of $600,000. An early estimate on proceeds was $40,000 with a record-breaking $6,578 from the opportunity drawing. Way to go, past president Jim Hughes!

Camp Enterprise, March 26–28

Speaker Valerie Jacobs of the Jacobs Family Foundation gave an inspirational speech at Camp Enterprise, chaired by Chuck Pretto, about her parents, who emigrated from Lebanon. The Jacobs Family Foundation was created in 1988 when Jacobs' father, in collaboration with his wife and three daughters, decided it was time to give back to the community. They invested in an economically underdeveloped community in southeast San Diego and Market Creek Plaza was born.

▲ Walkers gather for a walk around Mission Bay.

▲ Bonnie Schwartz and President Hartman warmed up for the popular walk around Mission Bay.

participated in the Club 33 Walk at Mission Bay. It was just a warm-up for the next Walks in February and May.

A Halloween round of golf at the San Diego Country Club brought the following results. Team low net: Linda Stirling, John Anewalt, Phil Gildred, and Sandy Purdon (130); low gross men: Tom Wilson (78); low gross women: Bonnie Schwartz (94); low net men: Marten Barry (71); and low net women: Bonnie Schwartz (74). Longest drive: Tom Wilson and Linda Stirling.

A full field of five groups played in the June 26th tournament at La Jolla Country Club. Bob Randall won the coveted Jack Thompson Memorial Trophy with a net score of 146,

▲ Grotarians enjoyed a wine-tasting event at Jackson Design and Remodeling.

edging out Marten Barry and Sandy Purdon by two strokes. The lady winners were Bonnie Schwartz (low gross), who also won the longest drive, and Linda Stirling (low net). Tom Gable captured the longest drive for men. Other results were low gross men: Tom Wilson, Don Tartre, and Bob Kelly; and low net men: Bob Randall, Don Tartre, and Vance Gustafson. Team winners were low gross: Roy Bell, Bonnie Schwartz, Tom Gable, and Tom Wilson; and low net: Jay Arnett, Vance Gustafson, Jim Reynolds, and Sandy Purdon.

Grotarian Events

Grotarians enjoyed a variety of events while getting to know each other. September found them enjoying a performance at the Balboa Theater, and later in the year, they toured SeaWorld. In between, they enjoyed a couple of wine-tasting events. A poolside chat hosted by Bill McColl took place in October, and a fireside chat was held at the home of Tom Vecchione.

Vision for the Future

Less than a month into the new Rotary year, a small group of the 2008–2009 Board of Directors met in the conference room to work out a Club 33 vision statement and continue work on the 2008–2013 Strategic Plan. Guided by Cindy Olmstead, the visioning team included Jack Anthony, Stan Hartman, Chuck Pretto, Suzy Spafford, Dick Troncone, and Executive Director Bruce Hunt.

Organizations Honor Club 33 Members

Barbara Bry, Judy Forrester, Bonnie Schwartz, and Linda Stirling received *San Diego Business Journal* "Women Who Mean Business" awards in October. Suzy Spafford was honored with an "Outstanding Celebrity Volunteer" award presented at the National Philanthropy Day luncheon on November 12. In January, Bink Cook received a "Four Avenues of Service" citation. The Cliff Dochterman Community Service Award was presented to Patti Roscoe and Steve Mueller in February.

In February, Ben Clay agreed to chair the upcoming Centennial Celebration.

▲ Thanks to Nancy Scott's enthusiasm in her "Muffy Upson" role, the crowd at the Diana Venable Auction was whipped into a buying frenzy!

▲ President Stan Hartman and Norbert Sanders visit with members of a local Rotary Club in Tijuana.

▲ President Hartman (right) and Jo Dee Jacob welcomed guest speaker Matthew Hervey, a member of the Price Charities Board of Directors.

Committees were to be formed and the celebration would kick off in June 2011. A prediction was made that Ben and his group would be very busy between now and then!

Linda Stirling made *Barron*'s "Top 1,000 Financial Advisors" list at number sixty. President Hartman was surprised with a mighty "Thank You!" and reward for all his work and support of the micro-credit program. The first Rotary Club 33 Achievement Award was presented in July to Paul Hartley, Jr. for recruitment of "a significant number of members and other good works."

It's official: in March, it was reported that Club 33 had the third largest membership in the world after Seattle, Washington (684), and Birmingham, Alabama (579).

There were two significant birthdays this year: happy ninetieth birthday to Walter Barrett (April 30) and ninety-fifth to Shelly Brockett (September 11), who is also the longest-affiliated member of Club 33. He joined in 1945!

Rotarians of the Quarter

Joyce Glazer
David Oates
Daryl Ferguson
Greg Zinser

New Members

NAME	PRIMARY SPONSOR
Roger Bailey, Strategic Transitions	Cheryl Wilson
Frank Baldwin, The Baldwin Group at UBS	Bill Gore
James Bayne, BB&T John Burnham Insurance Services	Jim Reynolds
Christopher Beach, La Jolla Music Society	Martha Dennis
Lisa Bruner, Alzheimer's Association, San Diego/Imperial Chapter	Sheryl Bilbrey
Lee Burdick, Higgs, Fletcher & Mack, LLP	Martha Dennis
Karen Cebreros, Elan Organic Coffees	Bonnie Schwartz
Philippe Cesson, CESSON	Rodney Moll
Michael Conner, Phoenix Water Management, LLC	John Sands
Paula A. Cordeiro, USD, School of Leadership and Education Sciences	Frank Arrington
Richard W. Cox, The Westgate Hotel	Bob Arnhym
Robert "Bruce" Drake, Boy Scouts of America	Pat Caughey
Ray Ellis, Ellis & Associates	Peg Eddy

(continued on next page)

(continued from previous page)

NAME	PRIMARY SPONSOR
Captain Thomas H. Farris, U.S. Coast Guard	Dennis Kenneally
Chandani Flinn, STAR/PAL	Kimberly Layton
Terry B. Grier, EdD, San Diego Unified School District	Tyler Cramer
George Guimares, Project Concern International	Tom Gable
Shandon Harbour, SDA Security	Rod Eales
Karen Hewitt, U.S. Attorney's Office	Andy Hewitt
Ann Hill, John D. Hill, MD, Inc.	Jo Dee C. Jacob
Todd Jackson, Jackson Design & Remodeling	Jim Groen
Michael Jones, Profinance Associates, Inc.	Susan Snow
David Kahn, San Diego Historical Society	Hal Sadler
Thomas Karlo, KPBS	Gloria Penner
Kevin Keenan, American Civil Liberties Union	Joe Craver
Ray King, Urban League of San Diego County	Joe da Rosa
Sheila Korn, Seniors at Home	Peg Eddy
Richard Kwiatkowski, San Diego Regional Airport Authority	Marlee Ehrenfeld
Walter Lam, Alliance of African Assistance	Roger Haines
Andy Liska, Abbene, Alcock & Liska, APC	Phil Blair
Linda Markiewicz, The Salvation Army	Joyce Glazer
Diane Martin, Sheffler & Martin, Inc.	Jeremiah Doran
Jennifer "Jen" Martino, Project X Media	Kobe Bogaert
Michael Meaney, Attorney at Law	Jan Driscoll
Timothy O'Brien, Stradling Yocca Carlson & Rauth	John Van Deusen
Anthony M. Palmeri, Yellow Cab of San Diego	Larry Stirling
Ake Persson, Sky Mobile Media, Inc.	Kobe Bogaert
F. Gregory Pyke, Best Best & Krieger, LLP	Bob Russell
T. D. Rolf, Studley, Inc.	Mario Bourdon
Carol Summerhays, DDS	Lisa Miller, MD
Heather L. Rosing, Klinedinst, PC	Joan Friedenberg
Ruth Sandven, Communications Plus	Neal Schneider
Roberta Spoon, Brodshatzer, Wallace, Spoon & Yip	Fred Baranowski
David Wescoe, San Diego City Employees' Retirement System	Martha Dennis
John H. Wilson III, Timken Museum of Art	Derrick Cartwright

HONORARY MEMBERS

Yvonne Larsen

Beatriz A. Valencia

PROGRAMS

Military

The program year started with Brigadier General Angela Salinas, commanding general of MCRD and the Western Region and the first woman to have that post. In August, Rear Admiral David Thomas, commander of a Joint Task Force on Guantanamo, spoke about the base and how it was run. He provided a fascinating look behind the scenes of something that was very much in the forefront of the news.

On September 11th, Club 33 celebrated Fleet Week. The luncheon was chaired by Steve Cushman and many special guests were spotted as the Club honored reservists and their employers. Bill Dick gave a thoughtful message inspired by the seventh anniversary of 9/11.

Sports

Sports-oriented programs included Jim Steeg, executive vice president and chief operating officer of the Chargers, who talked about his off-field service activities during the year. In 1995, Alex Spanos created the Chargers Community Foundation, which has been a leader in supporting causes critical to the community. The foundation quietly supports numerous causes, including charities, education programs, law enforcement, youth and youth sports, Special Olympics, homeless shelters, senior centers, medical centers—and the list goes on. It was noted that the Chargers Blood Drive is now in its thirtieth year.

In October, Club 33 welcomed Olympians Mike Hazle and Stephen Strasburg, a bronze medal winner, who told of their experiences in Beijing. The annual Holiday Bowl program in December featured Bruce Binkowski, executive director, and Mark Neville, associate director.

Health

Local health organizations were featured during the year. Dr. Wendy Levin presented a fascinating program in September. As associate director of Oncology Translational Medicine for Pfizer Global Research & Development, Levin leads a team that studies the future of medicine and treatments.

In November, Club 33 member Dr. Richard Coutts kicked off the PolioPlus campaign. In another example of "six degrees of separation," the audience learned that President Hartman's wife and mother-in-law were both treated by Hartman's dad for polio long before Hartman met his bride-to-be. Dr. Coutts, the District 5340 point person, reported that Club 33 led in donations with nearly $213,920!

In May, Club 33 welcomed Pam Smith of the San Diego County Aging and Independence Services agency.

Local Programs

A wide variety of programs covered local and regional topics and Club 33 members appreciated being updated on matters of civic importance. The club heard from Ray Ashley, Maritime Museum; Craig Blower, Ruben H. Fleet Science Center; Peter MacLaggan, Poseidon Resources Corporation, regarding the Carlsbad Desalination Project; the CCDC, regarding the proposed civic center; the City of San Diego Commission for Arts and Culture; the chairman of the Board of Port Commissioners; the San Diego County Water Authority; the Metropolitan Transit Authority; and SANDAG. An April meeting took place at the San Diego Zoo, which included a tour of the new Elephant Odyssey and the exciting news of a brand-new baby giraffe born that day.

A riveting program was presented in October by U.S. Attorney and Rotarian Karen Hewitt. She spoke of trends in federal prosecutions in the Southern District of California and the status of the U.S. border.

Education

Terry Grier, superintendent of San Diego City Schools, brought an update on the local schools. In addition, Club 33 heard from the executive director of Barrio Logan College Institute and Dean Paula Cordeiro, School of Leadership and Education Sciences at the University of San Diego.

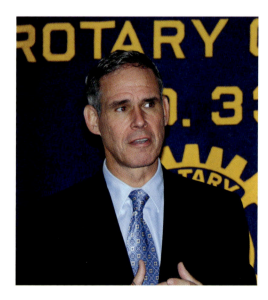

▲ Dr. Eric Topol, a chief academic officer at Scripps Health, described the "Well-derly Group," eighty-plus-year-olds with no health problems. Topol headed the team that discovered the gene that makes people susceptible to heart attacks. If those codes are discovered early in life, people can change their habits to reduce the risk of heart attacks!

◂ Reo Carr (far right) moderated the October "Point-Counterpoint" between city attorney candidates Jan Goldsmith (left) and Mike Aguirre. At the end of the debate, President Hartman presented each candidate with a Rotary coin with the Four-Way Test stamped on one side and asked that they keep it on their desks.

◂ Guest speaker Richard Dreyfuss.

◂ T. Boone Pickens and President Hartman.

◂ President Hartman and Richard Dreyfuss.

Other programs during the year featured Larry Prior, the CEO of SAIC, who spoke on national security, critical infrastructure, energy, environment, and healthcare, and Dan Walters, who shared his usual insightfulness from his perch as a *Sacramento Bee* columnist, presenting "Is California Really Ungovernable?"

Richard Dreyfuss arrived not as a movie star, but as a concerned citizen who talked about civics and questioned why it is no longer taught in schools. He described his mission: to do what he can to reinstate the teaching of civics. An April meeting brought T. Boone Pickens, who spoke about The Pickens Plan to end the United States dependence on foreign oil.

Programs Also Entertained and Inspired

In July, longtime member Pat Crowell shared memories from his yearlong European trip, which covered 27,000 miles and twenty-four countries. He shared some of the 13,000 slides he took during the year.

John Boland, chief content officer for National PBS, spoke in November about

▲ Marvin Hamlisch.

the nation's 355 public broadcasting stations. Dr. Kazuo Inamori, founder of Kyocera Corporation and the Kyoto Prize, came in March and brought three Kyoto award-winners. Sandi "Joy is an Inside Job" Kimmel entertained and inspired at the April Staff Appreciation Day Program. Another April treat was Marvin Hamlisch's appearance. No matter the venue, his storytelling and piano playing always delight!

Club 33 is fortunate to have so much talent among its members. Often the meetings featured the talents of Tom Blair, Joyce Gattas, Steve Hubbard, Patti Roscoe, Suzy Spafford, Geri Ann Warnke, and a host of others. The much-anticipated Holiday Luncheon and Sweethearts Day luncheon showcased members in a very big way.

Later in the spring, Larry Bock spoke about the upcoming Science Festival, which he founded.

In June, Ples Felix and Azim Khamisa shared a jaw-dropping program about forgiveness and hope. Felix's grandson, Tony, shot and killed Khamisa's son, Tariq. Khamisa founded the TKF Foundation based on teaching forgiveness. The first person he enlisted was the grandfather of his son's killer. Together they teach peace and non-violence to kids.

MacLaggan Award

▲ Dr. Fred Frye presented the MacLaggan Award to Club 33 member Michael Brunker.

▲ The MacLaggan Award was presented to Dr. Richard Kelly by Dr. Fred Frye.

Holiday Luncheon

◢ *Jo Dee "Rudolph" Jacob made an appearance at the annual Holiday Luncheon.*

Salute to Local Heroes, January 15

Police Chief Bill Landsdowne noted that Isaac Mendez was honored at the Salute to Local Heroes for coming to the aid of a sexual assault victim. Angela Williams followed and got the license plate number of a suspect who shot at an SDPD officer. Chief Deputy DA Dan Lamborn told of Sylan Dearborn, who chased and caught a DUI hit-and-run suspect. Also honored were Deon Millan and Dejion Rivers, who stopped a hatchet attack. Sheriff Bill Kolender described the actions of Charlton and Alexandra Lee, who aided and saved a stabbing victim. President Hartman presented the Organization Award to Bud Silva, president of the Honorary Deputy Sheriffs' Association.

Economic Forecast, January 8

At the annual Economic Forecast luncheon, Bill Holland predicted the Dow Jones Industrial Average would close at 10,000 and Linda Stirling's prediction was 10,500. The Dow closed on December 31, 2009, at 10,428.

◢ *The annual Economic Forecast luncheon.*

Ms. San Diego: Yvonne Larsen

Honored for numerous philanthropic and humanitarian causes, the new Ms. San Diego was president of her senior class at Hoover High School and earned a scholarship to attend SDSU. She has presided over

the Rady Children's Hospital Auxiliary and the Sharp Healthcare Foundation. According to the *Union Tribune*, she played a big part in the growth of the San Diego Zoo, and the Zoo sent some special representatives to the Rotary luncheon, including a cheetah—with a companion dog—and a playful Malaysian binturong, or bearcat. The cheetah looked like she had just finished a meal, or perhaps was anticipating one.

◢ *Mayor Jerry Sanders presented the Ms. San Diego plaque to Yvonne Larsen.*

Fleet Week, September 11

Chair: David Oates

◢ *The Marine Corps color guard opened the annual Fleet Week luncheon.*

◢ *Fleet Week head table.*

▲ In August, District Governor Pam Russell visited Club 33 and was welcomed by Amnon Ben-Yehuda (left) and former executive director Chet Lathrop.

▲ RI President Dang-Kurn Lee visited Club 33 on January 22, 2009. Two Rotary physicians, past president Tom Vecchione (left) and Richard Coutts, welcomed him.

THE ROAST

Stan' By Your Man!

Escorted in to the sounds of "Hail to the Chief," Stan was led to the stage and sat down on an old beat-up wooden desk on which sat a feebly shining shadeless lamp. Next, the Synchronized Precision Insurance Team (a.k.a. SPIT) combined marching skills with briefcases, money, contracts, the IRS, and the SEC. Other stars included Nancy Scott as Muffy Upson and Craig Blower as her butler, Jeeves. The Club 33 Singers sang "Yada, Yada, Yada" to the tune of ABBA's "Money, Money, Money," a nice rendition of "Try to Remember," and the Beatles' "Help." Geri Warnke, in blond wig and silver go-go boots, brought the house down with her version of "Stan' By Your Man," a la Tammy Wynette. The final Club 33 song was "Fifty Ways to Say it's Over" to help Stan conclude his term.

Stan responded with gracious thanks to his family; all the members of Rotary, the board, and committees; and staff members Bruce, Margaret, and Pauline. Concluding in grand style, the audience gave a richly deserved standing ovation to their man, Stan!

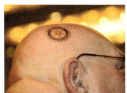

▲ Top: President Hartman and unofficial club portraits.

▲ Above: The Rotary logo has turned up in all sorts of unusual places.

129

CHAPTER NINE

Richard A. Troncone

2009–2010

"Give the Gift of Rotary."

CHANGE OF COMMAND

Installed on July 2, 2009, Richard A. "Dick" Troncone quickly took command and exercised his "presidential prerogative" to give the inspirational moment himself. In keeping with the upcoming Fourth of July, he delivered an inspirational message titled "America, the Land of Opportunity," penned by his mother in 1928 for her naturalization ceremony. Then Suzy Spafford and George Harris led the audience in "God Bless America!" Mayor Jerry Sanders, longtime friend and fraternity brother of Troncone, administered the oath of office in front of Troncone's family, friends, and fellow Sigma Alpha Epsilon fraternity brothers.

He began his remarks by thanking the late Bob Cleator, Sr., Bob Cleator, Jr., and Dick Green for "giving him the gift of Rotary" by sponsoring him into Club 33 in 1984. As the one-hundredth president of Club 33, Troncone then listed an ambitious array of priorities for the year ahead: membership, with an emphasis on younger members; programs, featuring local and state issues and club history; club finances, finding ways to counteract funding cuts after the losses in our endowment; and

PolioPlus, continuing the program begun by past president Stan Hartman.

Mayor Sanders gave an update on his focus for the year for the city, which included the Balboa Park Centennial in 2015, a new downtown library, a new civic center complex, convention center expansion, Lindbergh Field issues, and re-engagement with the Chargers. Talk about an ambitious list for both leaders! Troncone adjourned his first meeting ten minutes early, presumably to get started on those goals!

⬦ Mayor Jerry Sanders (left) inducted new President (and fraternity brother) Dick Troncone.

⬦ John Mehnert and Joe Flynn at the "Christmas You Missed."

SERVICE ABOVE SELF

The Veterans Village Stand Down in July was held on the grounds of San Diego High School. In addition to members' contributions of towels, washcloths, and other supplies, countless hours of volunteer time were recorded by Rudi Brewster, Lyle Butler, Mike Caruso, Mike Conner, Mickey Flynn, David Oates, Steve Oggel, Bob Russell, Dick Sullivan, Marc Tarasuck, and Executive Director Bruce Hunt. The first Stand Down event was held in 1988 in San Diego. Now there are approximately 300 held annually throughout the nation.

In July, twenty-seven committee chairs reported that Club 33 had 343 committee volunteers who gave 8,569 hours of service to 4,992 individuals. In addition, $113,560 in grants was given to various organizations. The annual Club 33 fishing trip was held in September, with the "catch" distributed, as always, in January by the Fish Across the Border Committee.

In November, Rotarians painted and repaired an elementary school at the Tecate Work Day.

Although snow doesn't often affect San Diegans, this year Mother Nature provided a

⬦ Rotarians gathered in Tecate for the annual World Community Service Day.

West Coast blizzard, which cancelled hundreds of flights and forced members of the armed services to bivouac in the USO lounge at the airport. Club 33's Military Affairs Committee helped distribute food and beverages to those who were on their way home for holiday visits. Since the travelers had no place to go, sturdy volunteers kept the USO open twenty-four hours!

The MOST team held a clinic in Tijuana at Hospital Ingles in February and corrected the congenital anomalies of forty-three children. The Tijuana Rotary Club Central 100 helped the team with patient transport, meals, and fellowship. In April, the forty-member team took a weeklong trip to Huejutla de

▲ Rotarians at Work Day included (from left) Jan Driscoll, President Dick Troncone, Geri Warnke, and Garrett Clark.

▲ Rotarians at Work Day was promoted by Andy Fichthorn (left) and Michelle Candland. George Alexander looked on from the head table.

▲ Colin Wied, Dennis Kenneally, Bob Russell, and Mike Rowan at Ft. Rosecrans for Rotarians at Work Day.

Reyes, a two-and-a-half-hour bus journey southwest of Tampico, Mexico. During the week, nearly 300 children were helped.

The annual Rotarians at Work Day took place in April. Chaired by Tom Gehring with the able assistance of vice chair Robert Borgman, Joe Austin, and Michelle Candland, many projects were successfully completed.

MEMBERSHIP

Fellowship, Camaraderie, and Engagement

One of the first major actions of the new year was the approval of the revised constitution and by-laws for Club 33, something that had been under way for several years and had not been undertaken since the club's founding in 1911.

Many, many hours went into this, and special thanks were given to Tyler Cramer, Peter

Duncan, Al Harutunian III, Sandy Mayberry, and Bob Russell. They focused their legal minds on the current documents and determined what revisions needed to be made based on current California state law, how the club conducts business, and day-to-day operations. The changes to both documents were approved by the membership. Another important change was to add the position of "president nominee" in the election roster. The position would debut in the 2010–2011 Rotary year.

Fun and Fellowship

The annual Day at the Races resulted in fun, but no official word on losers or winners (except, of course, the horses!). The August 20

Diana Venable Auction, December 10, 2009

The Club 33 Auction Committee was led by co-chairs Jo Dee Jacob and Marc Tarasuck. Thanks to their hardworking committee and the opportunity drawing run by Jim Hughes, which produced $5,288, additional gifts and matches brought the total to $10,576. Mike Hogan conducted the live auction, which raised $12,000 on eight items in fifteen minutes! The highlight of the day was the "Kiss the Pig" contest, the brainchild of Ellen Casey. The contest winner was the Rotarian who raised the most dollars and, although hotly contested by Dick Green and Nancy Scott, Dick Green emerged victorious and puckered up with the precious porcine. Rotarians will do just about anything to support the Diana Venable Scholarship Fund, which was $45,000 richer as a result!

▲ *President Troncone at the Diana Venable Auction with scholarship candidates Sherron Garrett and Sandy Sophal.*

▲ *A highlight of the Diana Venable Scholarship Fund Auction was the Kiss the Pig Contest. Dick Green watched as Nancy Scott and Elmer puckered up.*

Camp Enterprise, April 15–17

For the thirty-fifth year of Camp Enterprise, Wayne Goodermote was the chair of the committee which consisted of Craig Blower, Michelle Candland, Peg Eddy, Sandy Mayberry, and Wes Wilmers.

Speaker Bill Walton spoke to the club for the first time in over twenty-five years. In spite of thirty-six orthopedic surgeries, he "keeps getting back on the bus." He gave credit to those who impacted his life: his parents and UCLA Coach John Wooden, who guaranteed that Walton would be with first-class players and first-class human beings. Also in the audience were Rocky Graciano and his wife.

▲ *Camp Enterprise guest speaker Bill Walton visited Club 33 for the first time in over twenty-five years.*

Padres game was a great evening of fellowship and hot dogs in spite of the Padres' 5-1 loss to the St. Louis Cardinals. The annual Rotary fishing trip in September and tennis outings in October and May satisfied the athletic desires of some Club 33 members. Sixteen elite tennis players gathered at the Barnes Tennis Center in May for the final match. Vern Aguirre and Manu Daryanani won against Jim Groen and Brian Pyke. Looks like there were some "ringers" in the group!

Golfers enjoyed a November outing at the San Diego Country Club. The first-round leader was Dick Green (73), followed by Bob Jacobs (74) and Marten Barry (76). Bonnie Schwartz won both low gross and net for women. Twelve golfers teed up in March at the San Diego Country Club. Dick Green maintained his lead with a cumulative score of 144. In the ladies category, Bonnie Schwartz won low gross, low net, and the longest drive. The putting contest resulted in a three-way tie between Dick Green, Ben Haddad, and Bonnie Schwartz. The third and final round of the Club 33 Championship was held on June 2 at the La Jolla Country Club. The golfer with the lowest net score for two of the three rounds would become the club champ, which was Dick Green with net scores of 71 and 73. However, a new rule that

▲ Jay Arnett looked on as Bob Fletcher and a guest landed some big ones on the annual Rotary fishing trip.

▲ Tennis players (from left): Bonnie Schwartz, Vern Aguirre, Bruce Hunt, and Peter Baekkelund.

President Troncone played a prank at the April 1st Club 33 meeting.

Woody Ledford, Geri Warnke, and President Troncone enjoyed a walk around Mission Bay.

required attendance at all three events caused Green to be disqualified. (Just kidding, he actually won!) Tom Wilson won the longest drive award. In May, Don Tartre reported that he shot his age on the golf course: 75. Go, Don!

The meeting on April 1 was nearly brought to a standstill when President Troncone, responding to critical remarks from his ever-vocal brother-in-law, Dick Green, abandoned the podium and walked out. Fortunately, Dick (Green, that is) assumed the podium and carried on. The April Fool's Day prank was later revealed. That president is such a card!

Members in the News

Nominees for *San Diego Business Journal*'s annual "Women Who Mean Business" awards in October were Club 33 members Jan Cetti, Peg Eddy, Jen Martino, and Judy Thompson. Ann Hill was named "Outstanding Organizational Volunteer" at the National Philanthropy Day luncheon on November 15th. The spring LEAD San Diego awards were presented to Nikki Clay, "Graduate of the Year," and Jim Mulvaney, who received

the Morgan Award. Chandani Flinn received the Betty Peabody "Non-Law Enforcement Community Award" from San Diego County Crime Stoppers. Jim Groen and Todd Jackson, Jackson Design & Remodeling, received another prestigious award to add to their growing collection!

In other news, Ben Clay and Sandy Mayberry, co-chairs of the upcoming Club 33 Centennial, added Joyce Glazer and Craig Evanco to their committee. Troy Sears offered to sail America's *Stars & Stripes* for a contribution to the Coast Guard Relief Fund. On February 4th, the Academy Leadership Award was presented by District Governor Marge Cole to Bonnie Schwartz and Chuck Pretto. Darlene Davies was appointed chair of the San Diego County Commission on the Status of Women.

Mayor Jerry Sanders proclaimed May 1 as "Suzy Spafford Day." Councilman Todd Gloria presented the proclamation at the May Day event at the Marston House. Among the events and exhibits, many geraniums were featured, including varieties named for Suzy's Zoo characters. Chuck

Pretto received the Rotary International "Four Avenues of Service" citation for "leadership in so many Club 33 activities." Special thanks were given to Pretto, who donated a computer to a physician in Malawi, and Roy Lange was congratulated for thirty-eight years of perfect attendance. The Cliff Dochterman Award was presented to Mike Rowan and Bill McColl. The late Dr. Homer Peabody was inducted in the San Diego Tennis Hall of Fame.

▲ President Troncone presented a Paul Harris Fellowship to Carolyn McCormick, who joined Club 33 in 2009.

Rotarians of the Quarter

Richard Coutts, MD

Craig Blower

Joe Craver

Larry Showley

Board of Directors, 2009–2010

Richard A. Troncone, President

Bonnie Schwartz, President-elect

Stanford F. Hartman, Jr., Past President

Andrew W. Hewitt, Secretary/Treasurer

Barbara "Bink" Cook

Tyler W. Cramer

Wayne K. Goodermote

Richard M. Green, DPM

Albert T. Harutunian III

Jo Dee C. Jacob

Sandra L. Mayberry

Lisa S. Miller, MD

Charles J. Pretto

Robert G. Russell, Jr.

Suzanne "Suzy" Spafford

New Members

NAME	PRIMARY SPONSOR
Carolyn B. McCormick, Belsky & Associates	Don Balfour
Bradford Barnum, AGC	Joanne Pastula
Bradford Bates, Habitat for Humanity	Jim Groen
Robert Bauchman, Northern Trust, NA	Garet Clark
James Buley, Buley Wealth Management Group	Mike Morton
Jason Burns, Profits 4 Purpose	Ed Ecker
Paul Byrne, ReadyTECH	Jeremiah Doran
Larry Clemens, San Diego Housing Commission	Larry Stirling
Sandi Cottrell, Art Walk San Diego	Patti Roscoe
William T. Earley, Luce, Forward, Hamilton & Scripps	Al Harutunian III
Edward Ecker, Give Something Back Business Products	Jen Martino
Christina Elliott, LPE, Inc.	Jen Martino
Ian Falcon, Araya Staffing	Matt Hom
Jeffrey Fisher, Cox Media	Phil Blair
Rick C. Gentry, San Diego Housing Commission	Andrew Poat
Melanie Gordon, gWave Consulting, Inc.	Jen Martino
M. Ray Hartman III, DLA Piper, LLP	Stan Hartman
Keith B. Jones, Ace Parking	Ben Clay
Bruce Knowlton, Moss Adams, LLP	Ed Kitrosser
Sarah Lamade, Space and Naval Airfare Systems Command	Bink Cook
April Langwell, Federal Bureau of Investigation	Stan Hartman
Nick Macchione, Health and Human Services Agency, County of San Diego	Bill Gore
Scott Maichel, AmCheck	John Van Deusen
Peter J. MacCracken, Strategic Communications	Marlee J. Ehrenfeld
Irene McCormack, San Diego Unified Port District	Ben Clay
Jackie Meyer, Qualcomm, Inc.	Marlee J. Ehrenfeld
Michael A. Morton, Jr., Brigantine Family of Restaurants	Mike Morton, Sr.
John Ohanian, 211 San Diego	Joe Craver
Serhat Pala, TestCountry	Kobe Bogaert
Todd Poling, Vantage Point Advisors, Inc.	Keith McKenzie
Jenni Prisk, Prisk Communication	Judy Thompson
Michael Rosenberg, La Jolla Playhouse	Martha Dennis
Gary Shaw, San Diego Convention Center	Bob Witty
Robert E. Smith, General Dynamics NASSCO	Phil Blair
Tracy Sundlun, Competitor Group/Elite Racing	Paul Nestor
Robert Vosskuhler, Clinical Research Partners	Bill Herrin
Glenn Younger, Grah Safe and Lock	Michael Jones

HONORARY MEMBER
Elena L. Salsitz, Honorary Consul of the United Kingdom

In Memoriam

Robert Breitbard

Herman Gadon, PhD

Warner L. Harrah

James W. Hughes

Christine Nietfeld

Ralph A. Thompson

Grotarian Events

The first Grotarian event of the year was at the Museum of Natural History. Sixty Rotarians and guests toured the "Body Works" exhibit. John Morrell organized the event and docents included physicians Doug Arbon, Richard Coutts, Richard Sullivan, and Tom Vecchione. A September poolside chat was held at the home of John Morrell, and November found the group enjoying an evening at Solana Beach. A February tour of the new SDSU Alumni Center was followed by the women's basketball game. Watching the Lady Aztecs defeat the TCU Lady Frogs 84-61 capped off the evening.

Additional events included a March 25th Sundowner and an April evening of fun and food at Phil's BBQ. The last event of the year was in June, when Grotarians and guests enjoyed a private tour and reception at the Timken Museum.

▲ *Chandani Flinn and a very tall friend at a Brown Bag Luncheon at the San Diego Zoo.*

PROGRAMS

San Diego

In keeping with the tradition of presenting programs touting various aspects of living in "America's Finest City," the Program Committee had numerous hits during the year. Don Kent, the president of Hubbs-SeaWorld Research Institute, brought news of the remarkable things being done to increase fish production. His programs featured facts and figures regarding the importance of California's annual $100-million recreational and commercial fishing industry.

In March, Tom Gable shared a video that told the story of how public relations contributed to the growth of San Diego over the last fifty years. He also spoke about the transformation of downtown San Diego and redefining the city as "America's Finest City" (thanks to former governor Pete Wilson!). Other success stories included the San Diego Zoo, SeaWorld, and the Chargers. Mary Schmidt-Krebs and Donna Alm, both experienced PR professionals, shared additional public relations success stories.

Additional programs included Ruben Barrales, president and CEO, San Diego Regional Chamber of Commerce; Paul Steffens, executive director, Armed Services YMCA; Ed Moss, president and publisher, *Union Tribune*; Chris Cramer, chairman of the board, Convention Center Corporation; and Deborah Reed, CEO, SDG&E, who brought encouraging news about energy, clean homes, and smart meters.

A July program featured a lively debate about Lindbergh Field. Speaking in favor of "Destination Lindbergh" was Jim Panknin, board member of the San Diego Regional Airport Authority. Speaking against it was Bob Kittle, editorial page editor of the *Union Tribune*, who referred to the plan as "Destination Hindenburg." The debate will go on.

In March, the ever-popular KPBS Editors Roundtable, moderated by Gloria Penner, featured Scott Lewis, *Voice of San Diego*; Barbara Bry, *San Diego News Network*; and Dr. John Warren, *San Diego Voice and Viewpoint*. The discussion covered local political races, ballot measures, and education. It was broadcast the next day.

At the July 30th Club 33 meeting, SDSU Head Basketball Coach Steve Fisher predicted that the team would make the Sweet Sixteen

in next year's NCAA tournament. Although the men's team didn't make that goal, the SDSU Women's Basketball team was part of the Sweet Sixteen line-up in March 2009. They won the first-round game against DePaul 76-70, but sadly, the Lady Aztecs lost the second-round game to Stanford 77-49.

Another local sports figure, Jeff Moorad, the new chief executive officer and minority owner of the Padres, visited Club 33 in August. Moorad requested community and fan support as changes took place over the "challenging and frustrating season." He told of the investment the team had made by signing nineteen of their twenty draft picks. On a lighter note, he spoke of sitting in a different seat each day in Petco Park and saying, "WOW!" The audience agreed. On April 29th, the Padres were in first place in their division.

Turning to legal issues, Club 33 heard from a variety of people who shared insider views. Rotarians welcomed Gary Schons, senior assistant attorney general for the state of California, and FBI special agents Erin Phan and Lamont Siller, who spoke about the downfall of ex-congressman Duke Cunningham. Rotarian Kevin Enright, presiding judge of the County of San Diego, gave a stellar program, and Paul Greenwood, deputy district attorney and director of the Elder Abuse Unit, presented "Elder Abuse, the Silent Crime." In addition, Judge George W. Clark of the San Diego County Superior Court presented "Justice and Science: Trials and Triumphs of DNA Evidence."

Issues surrounding public education were discussed by SDSU President Stephen Weber and UCSD Chancellor Marye Ann

▲ Kyoto Prize winners Dr. Peter Grant and Dr. Rosemary Grant were introduced at the April 22nd meeting by Chair of the Day Robert Horsman (left) and Dick Troncone (right). The first husband and wife team to win the prize, they noted that 2010 is the United Nation's "Year of Biodiversity."

◢ Panel moderator Reo Carr (center) with UCSD Chancellor Marye Anne Fox and SDSU President Stephen Weber, who discussed educational issues of the day.

Fox. In addition, James Lanich, PhD updated Club 33 on high-performing public schools.

In the area of health news, Rotarians heard from Mike Sise, MD, Scripps Mercy Trauma Services; Mike Murphy, chief executive officer, Sharp Healthcare; Gail J. McGovern, president and chief executive officer, American Red Cross (national); Kelly Ferrin, gerontologist and longevity expert; and Camile Sobrian, president, Wireless-Life Sciences Alliance, who spoke about making the delivery of healthcare more efficient.

Science topics were deftly handled by Alison Alberts, the chief conservation officer at the San Diego Zoo, who spoke about the emerging field of biomimicry and a new way of looking at nature. San Diego's own Dr. Patrick Abbott of SDSU, an internationally renowned and sought-after media expert, presented an interesting program about past and future earthquakes.

Not shy about avoiding controversy, Club 33 heard two speakers who generated discussion and opposing opinions. In March,

◢ Past president Frank Arrington; Dr. Patrick Abbott, professor emeritus at SDSU; and President Dick Troncone.

Dr. Yaron Brook of the Ayn Rand Institute presented a thought-provoking program titled "The Morality of War," described by members as "provocative, challenging, offensive, infuriating, and bone-chilling." In April, John Coleman, founder of the Weather Channel in the 1980s, presented "Global Warming is a Scam." Coleman first arrived in San Diego in 1994. In his program, he insisted that the reports of rising temperature are results of manipulated data, that the earth is in a normal interglacial cycle, and we can look to the normal pattern of warming for another 6,000 years. Will the airport issues be resolved by then?

Favorite wordsmith Richard Lederer presented an April 1st program on "Cats and Dogs." Although it could have generated controversy between "cat people" and "dog people," it was another typically entertaining program that Lederer is so famous for… and that was no joke!

In addition to special programs saluting the military, a September program about Navy SEALs was enthusiastically received. Rear Admiral Gary Bonelli, deputy commander of the Naval Special Warfare Command, and Master Chief Brian Yarbro talked about what it takes to be a SEAL.

Club 33 members also looked beyond the neighborhood to global issues. Rev. Canon Mary Moreno Richardson of St. Paul's Episcopal Church spoke about the tragedy of human trafficking. Past district governor Steve Brown described his nine trips to Afghanistan. Ambassador Charles Shapiro, senior advisor of the Bureau of Western Hemisphere Affairs, spoke about "Poverty in Latin America." Dr. Eric Dinerstein from the World Wildlife Fund talked about ongoing efforts to save the wild tiger. He shared that 2010 is the Chinese "Year of the Tiger." Currently there are around 3,200 wild tigers in the world. Without conservation efforts, the population could well disappear by 2022, which will be the next "Year of the Tiger."

Other programs included Milton Ezrati of the Lord Abbot Investment Company, who spoke about growth and pitfalls in the future of the U.S. economy, and California State Treasurer Bill Lockyer, who brought an update of the "State of Our State." A wild and wacky presentation by Mel Stuart, the producer of *Willy Wonka and the Chocolate Factory*, delighted the audience. Winner of multiple Emmys, a Peabody Award, and an Oscar nomination, Stuart entertained with anecdotes, backstories, and film clips from the movie.

In October, Troncone brought back the Brown Bag Luncheon, which had been on hiatus for several years. Members had the opportunity to visit fellow Rotarians' places of business, including Chris Cramer's ever-popular Karl Strauss Brewery.

▲ President Dick Troncone welcomed SAE fraternity brother T. Boone Pickens, who spoke on his "Pickens Plan" designed to decrease America's dependence on foreign oil.

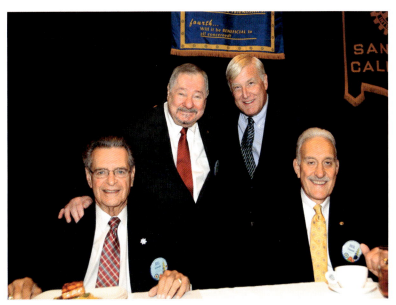

▲ The Sheriff Bill Kolender roast (from left): Bill Kolender, Bob Arnhym, County Supervisor Greg Cox, and President Dick Troncone.

In November, Club 33 had a "Roast and Toast" for Bill Kolender, who was retiring as sheriff of San Diego County. After fifty-three years of service in law enforcement, there were plenty of tales to be told. In spite of a warning that the "gloves might come off," the speakers really could not bring themselves to roast, and the program became more of a toast to the highly respected almost-retired sheriff. Other than a little good-natured ribbing, the program was about congratulations and admiration—or else people remembered that he still gets to carry a gun, even in retirement!

Mr. San Diego: Robert Payne, September 17

Paying tribute to Robert "Bob" Payne's vast involvement in San Diego, Mayor Jerry Sanders said he was surprised to learn that Payne was not already a "Mr. San Diego," and outlined his significant achievements in

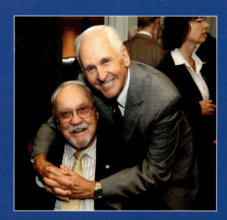

the food and hospitality industries, community service, and generosity to San Diego State. In return, Payne graciously paid tribute to Club 33's many service projects and spoke of his foundation, the L. Robert and Patricia L. Payne Family Foundation (located in San Diego), which focuses on youth, education, and medicine. He closed his acceptance with advice to "stay informed and add your voice."

▲ Robert Payne (right), 2010 Mr. San Diego, gave past president and 1986 Mr. San Diego Bruce Moore a big hug. Moore was president of Club 33 in 1975–1976.

Holiday Luncheon, December 17

More than thirty-five singers entertained at the Holiday Luncheon with the sounds of traditional holiday favorites and some new tunes. Members' kids and grandkids added their voices, and soloists provided

depth and meaning. The musicians were accompanied by pianist extraordinaire Bryan Verhoye and Colin Wied's La Jolla Brass. Adding musical notes were Paul Hartley III on guitar and Amnon Ben-Yehuda on violin. Over 450 attended, including one hundred very special senior guests. A merry time was had by all!

▲ A highlight of the annual holiday program is audience participation in "The Twelve Days of Christmas." From left, Rebecca Tuggle, Berit Durler, and James Buley act out "Five Golden Rings."

Economic Forecast, January 7

The panelists recapped last year's market activity by stating, "The recession is over, but nobody believes it; 2009 was the best year of the decade." Bill Holland's stock picks for 2010 were Boeing and Blackstone. Linda Stirling's were Johnson Controls and Tellabs. Don Bauder selected Callaway Golf and Wilmington Trust. Their predictions for a closing Dow Jones Industrial Average were Holland: 14,500 and Stirling and Bauder: 12,000. The Dow closed on December 31, 2010, at 11,578.

Salute to Local Heroes, January 14

At the Salute to Local Heroes, Sheriff Bill Gore honored Eric Sturhann, manager of a Poway bank, who experienced a bank robbery and followed the suspects in his car. As a result of Sturhann's actions, the bad guys were captured, pled guilty, and were removed from the streets. District Attorney Bonnie Dumanis introduced Blake Stech, who came to the aid of a woman being robbed and assaulted. Stech chased the assailants and ultimately testified against them. They were convicted and the victim recovered. Also honored was Julio M., a star witness in the gang execution of a police officer. He remained steadfast in his cooperation and testimony. The defendants were convicted and sentenced to life in prison. Police Chief Bill Landsdowne honored two individuals. Maurice Orange came to the aid of a robbery victim and

▲ *Salute to Local Heroes luncheon (from left): Police Chief Bill Landsdowne, Christina Henningan, Maurice Orange, District Attorney Bonnie Dumanis, Blake Stech, Julio M., organizational award-winner Gregory Meyer, and Bill Gore.*

chased the suspect for several blocks. He waited for the police to arrive and the suspect was taken into custody. Christina Henningan was attacked in the garage of her home by a suspect in six home invasion robberies. A marathon runner, Henningan chased him, and an off-duty border patrol agent heard her screams and held the suspect for police. The organization that received the Local Hero Award was the San Diego Regional Fraud Task Force, recognized for its very successful "Operation Bank Gig."

Sweethearts Day, February 11

Chaired by Marlee J. Ehrenfeld, Natasha Josefowitz shared words of wisdom at the Sweethearts Day luncheon and Ward Gill proudly touted the San Diego Symphony and its upcoming centennial year. A superb program consisting of the music of a violinist and a bassist from the Symphony delighted the audience. An especially haunting version of "Summertime" from Porgy and Bess ended the program.

Salute to Military, May 20

Service members from the Navy, Marines, and Coast Guard were honored at the May 20th meeting. Speaker Jerry Coleman (retired Marine Corps lieutenant colonel) described family, loved ones, and country as the keys to his life. He spoke about serving in both World War II and Korea, his career with the Yankees, and winning the World Series MVP Award in 1950. After announcing the names of the thirty award-winning military folks, Rotarians and guests saluted them with a standing ovation.

▲ *Jerry Coleman, USMC (Ret.) was the Speaker of the Day at the annual Salute to Military luncheon.*

Timeline

April 10 – Easter Sunday Earthquake
   The quake, which struck along the Laguna Salada fault line in Baja California, was felt more than 300 miles from the epicenter, and there were more than one hundred aftershocks in the twenty-four hours that followed.
March – Construction started on Terminal 2 at Lindbergh Field

THE ROAST

Dick "Don Alfonso" Troncone

In spite of his desire to "stay the course," Dick Troncone's year was eventful. July brought changes as new members began introducing themselves, and the Club History Minute was added to the news as a lead-up to Club 33's centennial. Social media became more prevalent as Club 33 traveled even deeper into the twenty-first century with a Facebook page and members were encouraged to sign up for LinkedIn

and Twitter. In April, the "Sick and Visiting" Committee became the "Get Well" Committee.

Meanwhile, back at the roast, gun-toting, sober-looking Rotarians escorted "The Don" into a room that had been transformed into a seedy motel room right out of a mobster movie. Pat Crowell's slideshow of "The Odd Father" was pronounced accurate in every way, and The Troncone Crime Family showed up en masse to say goodbye, including Mayor Jerry Sanders and SDSU President Steve Weber, who regaled the club with tales from The Don's college and fraternity days, not letting the truth stand in the way of a good story. Brother-in-law Dick Green was chosen to give a forty-year history of personal reflections, which ended with the conviction that the boss of the past year was a devoted, passionate, and quiet leader with a heart of gold. Pauline Hill presented the man of the hour with a new television set which, presumably, he will now have time to watch. The year ended quietly and safely.

On May 6th, Pauline Hill was honored with fifteen roses for her fifteen years of service as executive assistant to Club 33.

Past president Stan Hartman and almost-past president Dick Troncone share a moment at the podium.

"FBI Agents" Fred Baranowski and Mike Morton questioned The Don.

145

CHAPTER TEN

Bonnie Schwartz

2010–2011

> "*Gratitude is the best attitude.*"

◢ CHANGE OF COMMAND

Right off the bat (er, nine-iron), President Bonnie Schwartz laid out her BIG plans for the year: connections, thinking big, and connecting to the community through vocational service. But it didn't end there. The new prez had more huge plans up her golf shirtsleeve, and before the year was up, Club 33 would be hosting a first-time career awareness fair, the Large Club Conference (the first one in San Diego since 1979), and the inaugural Heilbron Awards. Time to get to work!

In July, the Pledge of Allegiance was re-instated as a formal part of the Club 33 meetings for the first time since the 1970s. Schwartz also began the practice of introducing the Rotarians who joined in certain decades. The 1940s were represented by Shelly Brockett (the club's most senior member, who joined in 1945). There were twelve members from the 1950s, twenty-one members from the 1960s, and fifty-one members from the 1970s. Members from the 1980s would be recognized in August.

A "Star Board" was established in October to feature the newest members and their sponsors. The goal this year would be to welcome fifty new members.

Schwartz concluded each meeting with her "Thought of the Week." It was so well received that she designed a journal with all the thoughts, which she presented at the end of her term to over fifty club members who contributed to the success of her term.

▴ Peter MacCracken with the Star Board.

▴ Mayor Jerry Sanders congratulated new president Bonnie Schwartz during the Change of Command luncheon on July 1, 2010.

▴ Peter Duncan presented the Diana Venable Scholarship Award to Ana Medina.

SERVICE ABOVE SELF

Starting the year off with service projects was the annual Stand Down for Homeless Vets held in July at a tent city set up on the San Diego High School campus. The Diana Venable Scholarship recipient, Ana Medina, appeared at the July 22nd Club 33 meeting. Another big event was the "Christmas You Missed," where nearly 600 moms, dads, and kids enjoyed the day.

Service projects ramped up in the fall starting with the September Club 33 fishing trip, aptly led by King Fish Bob Fletcher. First-time participant Chip Gordon caught the winning fish, a thirty-eight-pound yellowfin tuna.

Following up in January, the Fish Across the Border project provided 905 food baskets for needy families in Ensenada—along with the aforementioned tuna!

September found the MOST team in Mexico where Rotarian physicians Doug Arbon, Gene Rumsey, and Tom Vecchione

▴ The MOST team goes to Mexico (from left): Doug Arbon, MD, Gene Rumsey, MD, and Tom Vecchione, MD.

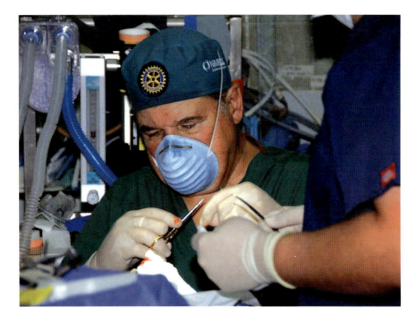

▲ Tom Vecchione, MD, in Mexico.

▲ Mike Caruso, Santa Claus (a.k.a. John Van Deusen), April Langwell, and Bob Russell paid a visit to the "Christmas You Missed" event.

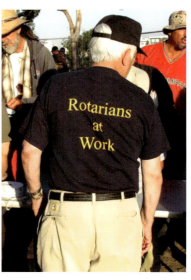

▲ In July, the annual Stand Down for Homeless Vets was set up in a tent city on the campus of San Diego High School. Mike Caruso modeled his "Rotarians at Work" T-shirt.

▲ Wilson Interact students with seniors at St. Paul's Villa.

performed thirty-nine life-transforming surgeries on children.

The holiday season included the news that Monarch High School would relocate to Barrio Logan, and the Military Affairs Committee was busy too. This year the group spent December 16th assisting with the Armed Services YMCA Super Parents Shopping Day. Mike Caruso led a pack

of busy elves including Rudi Brewster, Mike Conner, Wayne Goodermote, Paul Hartley III, Bruce Hunt, April Langwell, Cliff Myers, David Oates, Sandy Purdon, Bob Russell, and John Van Deusen, who all helped the junior enlisted military parents pick out gifts for their children. A real holiday surprise was the arrival of members of the Padres team to help with shopping—a treat for kids and their parents alike! The next day found Rotarians helping at the USO Hospitality Table at

Lindbergh Field, and six members spent Christmas Eve at the San Diego Homeless Veterans Winter Shelter passing out comfort items to the 160 residents.

The annual April Rotarians at Work Day, established by past president Jim Hughes six years ago, found 103 members participating in various projects around San Diego.

MEMBERSHIP

Fellowship, Camaraderie, and Engagement

In July, Payne Johnson reported on his very special eightieth birthday trip to France, where he revisited Normandy. Described as the "best birthday gift of a lifetime," Johnson was chosen to be the official American veteran to represent the 2010 Memorial Day by lowering the huge flag. Although it took ten people to fold and roll the flag, Johnson was asked to do the final three folds by himself and hold it alone for photographs.

Also in July, Richard Walker and John Van Deusen announced that they would soon be on Twitter—a great way to stay connected with other Rotarians. And by September, Club 33 was using LinkedIn for membership recruitment. The August 1 issue of the *Rotator* featured the first "Connections," a quarterly member profile featuring Vincent Mudd. In August, Schwartz spoke at the Naturalization Ceremony, hosted by Club 33, where 900 new citizens represented eighty-eight countries.

Career Awareness Fair, November 19

Chaired by Craig Blower, the sixteen committees under vocational service joined forces to bring a student population together to help the students investigate career paths. Also instrumental in the event were Phil Blair and Peter Bowie. Joe Austin, chair of the Business Department at San Diego High School, worked with teachers and students to determine a list of industries the students were most interested in. Based upon this information, Club 33 provided representatives from business, law enforcement, and the military. Each student could visit areas of interest for fifteen minutes, then report back to their teachers to analyze what they had learned about a particular industry. One hundred and twenty students participated in this first-time event.

MacLaggan Award, December 2

This year the MacLaggen Award was presented to Dr. Alan Shumacher for his exemplary lifetime of work with children. In addition to his activities with the Children's Advocacy Institute, the longtime pediatrician also served on the San Diego County Medical Society Board.

Diana Venable Auction, December 9

Chaired by Jo Dee Jacob, the membership was out in full force to participate in the Diana Venable Auction raffle and both live and silent auctions. The silent auction had all sorts of items, from handmade art to high-end golf bags. The live auction was so competitive that Chris Cramer and Irene McCormack offered to double up their auction items, and big thanks went to Jim Hughes, who generously matched the contributions. The auction raised a whopping $50,000! The fund now has $325,000 toward the $600,000 goal. Special guest speaker was Harvey White, philanthropist extraordinaire, who explained why he and his wife, Sheryl, have been so supportive of arts and education in San Diego.

Camp Enterprise, April 15

This year, chaired by Michelle Candland, seventy-five busy Rotarians hosted eighty-one high school juniors at Camp Enterprise, in Pine Valley. Young entrepreneur Noah Auerhahn, co-founder of Extrabux.com, was the speaker. In October 2010, Club 33 received the Vocational Service Award from Rotary International for Camp Enterprise.

Jim Haugh celebrated a significant birthday (ninety!) on August 28.

In September 2010, Club 33 was the third-largest Rotary Club in the world with 530 members!

Awards

Marlee J. Ehrenfeld won an Emmy to add to her collection and Jack Berkman was named to the PRSA College of Fellows. In October, Frank Arrington received a "Local Heroes" award from Bank of America's 2010 Neighborhood Excellent Initiative Awards and SDSU President Stephen Weber received the Copley Family YMCA 2010 Civic Tribute Award. November was a big month for Club 33-ers: Malin Burnham was named "Outstanding Fundraising Volunteer" at the National Philanthropy Day luncheon and the

San Diego Business Journal's "Women Who Mean Business" awards went to Rotarians Mary Walshok and Kathleen Pacurar. Darlene Davies was an honoree at the Junior League of San Diego Charter Day luncheon.

In April, Steve Cushman received the Gold Key Award from the local tourism industry and Patti Roscoe received the Lifetime Achievement Award from the special events industry.

Two of Club 33's attorneys were honored in the spring. Joan Friedenberg received the "Distinguished Citizen of the Year" award from the San Diego County Bar Association. *San Diego Magazine* named Sandy Mayberry as one of San Diego's best attorneys in the Family Law and Family Law Mediation categories.

This year, Rotary International presented three awards to Club 33 members. Bill and

Carol McDade received "Major Donor" recognition from Rotary International for their generous contributions. Wayne Goodermote received the Rotary International Avenues of Service Award.

In addition, the club earned an RI Presidential Citation with Distinction (one of thirteen of the sixty-one clubs in District 5340). Rotary Camp Enterprise received an RI Vocational Service Award. The first middle school Interact Club in District 5340 was the Wilson Tigers, and SDSU Rotaracts received a Presidential Citation.

Fun Stuff

The August Day at the Races found a few winners, but none big enough for fines.

Two Club 33 Walks around Mission Bay took place in October and May. In true Club 33 tradition, tennis and golf attracted a lot of interest and participation.

The End of Summer Tennis Tournament was held in September followed by a spring tournament. Kay North and Vern Aguirre were the winners. A donation of $296 from entry fees was given to the Youth Tennis San Diego Foundation.

The District 5340 golf competition found Don Tartre and Guy Maddox bagging some wins. Tartre won the low gross overall, low net flight, and closest to the pin on hole number nine. Maddox won closest to the pin on hole number five.

◢ Carol and Bill McDade celebrated five (!) Paul Harris Fellowships in honor of their five grandsons.

▲ Top: Rotarians and friends at the 2010 Fall Walk.

▲ Above: More golf: Bob Randall, Richard Carr, Bonnie Schwartz, and Guy Maddox.

The first Club 33 tournament round of the year was held on October 29th. Low gross scores were posted by Tom Wilson, Marten Barry, Jr., and Dick Green, respectively. Low net scores resulted in a three-way tie for first place by John Anewalt, Dick Green, and Marten Barry, Jr. (all with 73). The low net team honors (15 under) were shared by Bonnie Schwartz, Bob Randall, Richard Carr, and Guy Maddox.

In March, the golfers met at San Diego Country Club. Low net scores were recorded by Richard Coutts with a 69 for first place. John Anewalt and Dick Green, each with 71, tied for second place.

The ultimate round of the Club 33 Championship was held on June 3 at StoneRidge Country Club. Low net scores were Dick Green (73), Bob Kelly (74), and John Anewalt (76). Anewalt and Green tied for low net for the best two of the three rounds for the year at 144, forcing an eighteen-hole match play several weeks later. Green won 3-2, which made him the club champion for the year, and his name was placed on the club trophy once again!

In other social events, the inaugural event of the new "Society 33," chaired by

Jen Martino, was held on April 7th at Miguel's in Old Town. It was designed to promote friendship, social time, and networking. In May, the annual Jack in the Box "Hoops at the Beach" three-on-three basketball tournament on Mission Beach was held. Club 33 teamed up with other clubs in the district to underwrite the entry fees for twenty youth teams. This is the largest tournament of its kind in San Diego County. June Day at Rancho La Puerta, promoted by Nancy Scott, included gourmet cooking, fine wine, and spa treatments.

Rotarians of the Quarter
Mike Caruso
Judge Kevin Enright
Bob Fletcher
Leane Marchese

In Memoriam
E. Vaughn Lyons, Jr.
Oberlin J. Evenson
John P. Sands, MD
James F. Mulvaney
Arnold M. Silva
Gregg H. Wilson, DVM

Board of Directors, 2010–2011
Bonnie Schwartz, President
Wayne K. Goodermote, President-elect
Jo Dee C. Jacob, President Nominee
Richard A. Troncone, Past President
Tyler W. Cramer, Secretary/Treasurer
Warren J. Arnett, Jr.
Michelle Candland
Barbara "Bink" Cook
Joseph W. Craver
Albert T. Harutunian III
Joseph M. Horiye
R. Kendal Jones
Lisa S. Miller, MD
David B. Oates
Charles J. Pretto
Robert G. Russell, Jr.
Greg Zinser

New Members

NAME	PRIMARY SPONSOR
Craig Barrett, Barrett Engineering	Paul Hartley III
Josh Buchholz, NAI San Diego	Bob Fletcher
Kate Carinder, Scripps Mercy Hospital Foundation	Michael Sise
Michael Daniels, Real Estate Sales	Dick Green
David Detrick, Greystone Financial Group	Chris Sichel
Jon Fleming, Legacy Realty Capital, Inc.	Chris Christopher, Jr.
Matt Garrett, TGG Accounting	Keith McKenzie
Steven A. Green, MD, Sharp Rees-Stealy Medical Group	Don Balfour
Pamela Holden, CPA, BDO USA, LLP	T. D. Rolf
Gene James, Jack in the Box	April Langwell
Deidre Maloney, Momentum San Diego	Rebecca Pollock
Arnulfo Manriquez, Chicano Federation of San Diego	Ray Uzeta
Diana Marjip-Chuh, Nine Dragons, Inc.	Joe Horiye
Kevin McClintock, Goldfield Stage	Wayne Goodermote
Rick Mickels, American Relocation Services	Ed Ecker
Claudia Obertreis, Ability Center	Bonnie Schwartz
Kathleen Pacurar, San Diego Hospice & Institute for Palliative Medicine	Will Newburn
John Peelle, Peelle Financial Services	Lewis Linson
Holly Pobst, Crescent Geriatric Care Management, Inc.	Chris Sichel
Rebecca Pollock, Nielson Construction of California	Berit Durler
Deborah Ruane, San Diego Housing Commission	Richard Gentry
Doug Sawyer, United Way of San Diego	Peter MacCracken
Patrick Schultz, Ironstone Bank	Lisa Miller
Alan Spector, MD (Ret.)	Joyce Gattas
Eric Schwienfurter, Apex Contracting and Restoration	Glenn Younger
Pamela Stambaugh, Accountability Pays	Bonnie Schwartz
Joe Terzi, Convention & Visitors Bureau	Peter MacCracken
George W. Venables, U.S. Marshall Service (Ret.)	April Langwell
Gary Wang, SPAWAR	Sarah Lamade
Karin Winner, *Union Tribune* (Ret.)	Martha Dennis
Charlene Zettel	Andrew Poat

As of June 30, 2011, Club 33 had 511 members and twenty-two honorary members

---

Award Reception

▲ *Paul Harris Fellow Reception.*

▲ *President Bonnie Schwartz congratulated Norbert Sanders on his Paul Harris Fellowship.*

▲ *Bequest Society members (from left): Geri Warnke, Bink Cook, Jack Cook, Patti Roscoe, Joe Kennedy, MD, and Jim Tiffany.*

▲ *President Schwartz presented a service award to Woody Ledford.*

Grotarian Events

Grotarian events offered something for everyone from a July tour of Qualcomm Stadium to a January fireside chat at the home of Tom Vecchione. In between, there was a dinner at the Westgate Hotel in July featuring Bianchi wine and hosted by Richard Cox, Westgate's general manager, and in August, John Morrell hosted a poolside chat. September found several lucky Rotarians touring the USS *Jefferson City*, a *Los Angeles*-class attack submarine, based in Point Loma. In October, a group took a tour of Hill Hall on the campus of the University of San Diego, sponsored by Paula Cordeiro. Later on, a behind-the-scenes "Terminal to Tarmac" tour of Lindbergh Field led by Richard Kwiatkowski was both informative and entertaining. In December, Grotarians and guests were treated to an evening at the Cygnet Theater and a performance of *It's a Wonderful Life*. A February event at the Westgate Hotel organized by Richard Cox and two spring "sundowner" events, one at Luce Forward (hosted by Bill Earley) and another at the Higgs Fletcher and Mack offices (hosted by John Morrell), closed out a busy year for Grotarians.

PROGRAMS

At her first meeting, President Schwartz reinstituted the Pledge of Allegiance. Everyone agreed that it was a most welcome addition—the first time the Pledge had been a regular part of the meetings since the 1970s. Two authors appeared in July and August: Sarano Kelly, life coach and author of *The Game: Win Your Life in 90 Days*, and Bill Lerach, author of *Circle of Greed*. In September, Club 33 heard from Dr. Reese Halter, who presented a fascinating program on the connection between "Honeybees and Humans." Caressa Cameron, the current Miss America, delighted everyone, but especially the small troop of Girl Scouts who got to try on Cameron's tiara. Those girls left with service-oriented thoughts expressed by the lovely Miss America.

▲ Above left: Miss America Caressa Cameron chats up members of the local Girls Scouts of America.

▲ Above right: Past president and past district governor Bill McDade and President Schwartz enjoyed the District 5340 conference.

▲ Right: President Schwartz and the Badge Committee.

◢ President Schwartz with members of the Marine Corps Band.

◢ Jo Dee Jacob, Admiral Gary Roughhead, and President Schwartz.

◢ Guest speaker Steve Wampler.

In July, Club 33 members and guests were treated to the sounds of the Marine Corps Band. In August, Admiral Gary Roughhead of Commander Naval Operations (CNO) spoke. His presentation was preceded by music selections from the Navy Southwest Band. Later in the year, Club 33 welcomed former member

Major General Angie Salinas, USMC, who was visiting San Diego from her current assignment in Washington, D.C.

In January, Steven Wampler, a young man who was born with severe cerebral palsy, spoke to the club. In spite of overwhelming challenges, he was the first person with cerebral palsy to

◢ Irish Eyes smiled on everyone when the Club 33 Singers, with accompanist extraordinaire Bryan Verhoye and guest soloist San Diego Police Officer Gary Hassen, entertained at the March 17th meeting.

◢ The San Diego Chicken (a.k.a. Ted Giannoulas), guest speaker at the July 22nd meeting, took a shine to Joe Craver.

◢ Karen Winner, Judge Margaret McKeown, and President Schwartz.

scale El Capitan Mountain, the steepest sheer-faced mountain in the world. The husband and father of two established the Steven J. Wampler Foundation to give children with disabilities outdoor opportunities. What an inspiration!

Entertaining programs provided an often-needed respite in a busy day. This year several fell into that category. Ted "The San Diego Chicken" Giannoulas, who has entertained Elvis, The Beatles, and presidents Nixon, Ford, and Bush, was a popular visitor. Peter Yarrow dropped by in October and led the whole group in "This Land is Your Land." Nick Canepa, popular sports columnist at the *Union Tribune*, presented an interesting update on the San Diego sports scene. Tracy Sundlun presented a program about the wildly popular Rock 'n' Roll Marathon.

On March 17th, Irish eyes smiled on everyone. Steve Hubbard sang the popular Irish ballad "Mother Machree," and narrator Brian Patrick Michael Lange was escorted in by the Club 33 Singers. John Wilson of the Timken Museum of Art showed what was so special about Irish art, and Gary Hassen, San Diego police officer, sang "Danny Boy." To close, everyone joined in to sing "When Irish Eyes are Smiling."

June brought quite a variety of programs. Bob Gurr, a Disney Imagineer, spoke about working for the Disney organization. The Honorable Margaret McKeown spoke about the landmark case which led to admitting women into Rotary, and Honorary Member Pete Wilson spoke eloquently about the upcoming situation regarding Assembly Bill 190 and the release of felons into local counties. He did not paint a pretty picture.

Club 33 heard a variety of programs from agencies, organizations, and businesses in San Diego. Sheriff Bill Gore; Walt Ekard, the chief administrative officer of San Diego County; and Mayor Jerry Sanders each appeared with updates. Also presenting programs were SDSU President Stephen Weber and Lynn Reaser, an economist from Point Loma Nazarene University. Dan Gross, executive vice president of hospital operations, updated the group on Sharp Healthcare. Club 33 heard from Director Scott Anders of the Energy Policy Initiatives Center. Linden Blue, vice chair of General Atomics Aeronautical Systems, spoke about the San Diego firm's history and the technology advances that will change the world.

The cultural treasures of San Diego were not left out. Ian Campbell of the San Diego Opera and Sean Murray of Cygnet Theater brought information on current operatic offerings. In addition, a presentation on "Art Power" at UCSD gave Rotarians and guests even more to look forward to.

In political news, a debate was held regarding Proposition D on the upcoming ballot. Mayor Jerry Sanders argued in favor and City Councilman Carl DeMaio opposed. In February, California State Assemblyman Nathan Fletcher presented his perspective on Sacramento.

Looking out further from home, Club 33 heard from Jean Irwin, the 1989 Ambassadorial Scholar in England, and Matt Spathas of Sentre Partners, an organization that prepares students for the twenty-first century. David

▲ Steve Cushman, President Schwartz, and Nathan Fletcher.

▲ John Hawkins, President Schwartz, and Sheriff Bill Gore.

presented an interesting program about the Mongolian Plains, titled "Valley of the Khans Project." David Abney, the chief operating officer of the United Parcel Service, spoke with much insight on "Busting the Myths of Global Trade," and Jackie Freiberg presented "Blowing Doors off Business As Usual." By popular demand, Rotarian Mark Trotter reprised his "To Change the World" address that he gave at the Large Club Conference in February.

▲ President Bonnie Schwartz with the check for our centennial gift to the San Diego Symphony Music Education Program.

Shirk, PhD spoke about the U.S. immigration policy, and Alan Bersin, commissioner of U.S. Customs and Border Protection, also spoke to Club 33. In October, Dr. Albert Yu-Min, UCSD and *National Geographic*

Mr. San Diego: Joe Craver, October 14

Joe Craver was honored this year for a list of impressive accomplishments, not the least of which was the Purple Heart he received as an Air Force pilot in Viet Nam. He currently serves as chief executive officer of the American Red Cross San Diego Chapter. He also has been president of the Holiday Bowl, the Airport Authority, and a member of the board of Rotary Club 33. After accepting the award graciously and humbly,

he introduced the guest speaker, his son, Joe Craver III, who serves as president of SAIC's Infrastructure, Energy, Health and Product Solutions Group. In addition to talking about the $4-billion company, he spoke of the admiration he holds for his father and mother. Club 33 couldn't agree more!

▲ Joe Craver, Mr. San Diego 2010, with presenter Mayor Jerry Sanders.

Economic Forecast, January 6

San Diego's Voice of Wall Street, Bill Holland, said that 2010 was the best year on Wall Street in years. Linda Stirling, on the other hand, called 2010 a "year of fear," but shared that the fourth quarter showed solid improvement—employment was up, retail spending was up, and the S&P had a return of 50 percent. Her year-end prediction was 12,500. Bill Holland predicted 15,500. He recommended reading *The Big Short: Inside the Doomsday Machine* by Michael Lewis. The Dow Jones Industrial Average closed at 12,217 on December 30, 2011.

Salute to Local Heroes, January 20

Salute to Local Heroes began twenty years ago spearheaded by Bob Arnhym (this year's chair), Craig Evanco, and former executive director Chet Lathrop. Police Chief Bill Landsdowne presented the first award to SDG&E employee Daryl Hollins, who, from his sky bucket, observed a residential burglary in progress. He contacted the police, who responded and apprehended three armed suspects. Sheriff Bill Gore presented an award to Rachael Turner, the teenaged daughter of a Sheriff's Department lieutenant. She called a suspected child molester, pretending to be a girl he had allegedly molested years earlier. He confessed. The next award was awarded posthumously to Sharrel Blankenbaker, who sacrificed her life to save her grandchildren from being kidnapped at a Texas truck stop. The grandchildren she saved accepted the award on her behalf. Three final awards were presented by District Attorney Bonnie Dumanis to construction workers Mario Contreras, Steven Kane, and Carlos Partida, who chased a man they believed to have opened fire on a Carlsbad elementary school. When the man began to reload his weapon, the three held him down until police arrived. The organization award was presented to the San Diego Sexual Assault Felony Enforcement (SAFE) Task Force for their work in monitoring and investigating sex offenders in the community.

▲ Above: *Dr. Fred Frye presented the 2010 MacLaggan Award to Dr. Alan Schumacher.*

▲ Right: *Local Heroes presenters (from left): Sheriff Bill Kolender, District Attorney Bonnie Dumanis, and San Diego Police Chief Bill Landsdowne.*

THE ROAST

Bonnie Wins the Masters!

The lights dimmed and Bonnie Schwartz was escorted in by the past presidents preceded by Bruce Hunt with a large, tournament-style "QUIET" sign. The audience was magically transported to the Masters Golf Tournament in Augusta, Georgia. At the top of the leader board was Club 33's own Bonnie "Sports" Schwartz. Colorful commentary was provided against the background of historic photos and anecdotes. Clad in Masters green accentuated with golf gloves, hats, and props, the Club 33 Singers entertained with their own renditions of "She Is Bonnie" (borrowed from "I Am Woman") and "They Can't Take That Away From Me." And they didn't! Bonnie was *not* disqualified for moving her ball prior to marking it! After faux commercials and hearing backstories about Bonnie's college days, the audience was treated to seriously gracious lauds by Rudi Brewster, Patti Roscoe, Geri Ann Warnke, and Jean Young. Bonnie ended the day by thanking everyone, then thanking everyone again. The traditional gifts to Bonnie were highlighted by an official commemorative watch from the Masters in Augusta. The roast concluded. Badges were put away. Tables were cleared. But, the silhouette of Bonnie could be seen at the podium. She was still thanking people. Thank you, Bonnie. It was a very good year!

◢ Past presidents turn out for Bonnie's roast.

▲ Large Club Conference attendees. Front row (from left): Bruce Hunt, Mike Morton, Pauline Hill, Bill Gates, Sr., Claudia Johnson, Michelle Candland, Jenni Prisk, and Bob Fletcher; back row (from left): Jo Dee Jacob, Sandi Cottrell, Guy Maddox, Chuck Pretto, Paul Byrne, and Bill Earley.

Club 33 Hosts the Large Club Conference, January 20

On May 30, 2009, the Club 33 Board of Directors approved Executive Director Bruce Hunt's request to take its turn and host the Large Club Conference, the first time since 1979 that Club 33 hosted. Chaired by Mike Morton, Steering Committee members included Kobe Bogaert, Jo Dee Jacob, David Oates, Jenni Prisk, and Irene Wells. Others were Paul Byrne, Michelle Candland, Ed Ecker, Tom Gable, Claudia Johnson, Guy Maddox, and Chuck Pretto.

The four educational sessions were called "Waves" to give the conference a San Diego flavor. Jenni Prisk started Wave 1, "Planning." Her committee consisted of Sandi Cottrell, Bill Earley, and Paul Byrne. Wave 2, "Marketing," was led by David Oates and assisted by Darren Cecil, Chris Elliott, Steve Bond, Jen Martino, Todd Struyk, Ian Falcon, Valerie McCartney, and Scott Maichel. Kobe Bogaert produced Wave 3, "Membership," with the help of Jim Groen, Darren Cecil, Wes Wilmers, Bink Cook, Jen Martino, John Van Deusen, Don Teemsma, David Oates, and Mike Morton, Jr. Jo Dee Jacob caused Wave 4, "Development," and was helped by Merle Brodie and Jeanne Schmelzer.

Special thanks went to Bonnie Schwartz and her design firm, who produced all the graphics for the conference including the logo with its "Sun, Sailing and Surf-ice" tag

line as well as all signage in the hotel and on the cars used to pick up guests.

The highlight of the Large Club Conference was the keynote address by Bill Gates, Sr. As co-chair of the Bill and Melinda Gates Foundation, Gates has both the tools and insights to speak to world issues. He commended the PolioPlus campaign as a good example of how an international organization such as Rotary can leverage the work of medical research, community volunteers, and contributions from affluent nations to work toward the eventual eradication of this disease.

High praise was received from the 151 president-elect and executive director attendees.

Inaugural Heilbron Awards, June 23

The brainchild of President Bonnie Schwartz, the inaugural awards were presented at the June 23, 2011 meeting of Rotary Club 33. These awards, named for Carl Heilbron, the first president of Club 33, were designed to recognize companies that exemplify the "pay it forward" spirit by using their professional expertise via pro bono work to advance the well-being and success of others in the community. The chair of the Heilbron Committee was Karen Hutchens.

Exemplary Performance Awards were presented to Patti Roscoe for her service to the community and to Bill Davidson on behalf of Paul Jacobs for the work of

▲ Opposite: Heilbron Award winners. Front row, seated (left to right): Frank Urtasun, SDG&E, winner, Large Company class; representative of Crystal Pyramid Productions, winner, Small Company class; Patti Roscoe, winner, Exemplary Performance Award, Service to Community; Bill Davidson, Qualcomm, accepting on behalf of Paul Jacobs, Exemplary Performance Award, Company Service to Community; Tina Howe, Bill Howe Plumbing, winner, Medium Company class. Back row (left to right): Randy Frisch, president and publisher, *San Diego Business Journal*; Club 33 President Bonnie Schwartz; representative of ESET North America and Bruce Knowlton, Moss Adams, LLP, second- and third-place winners respectively, Medium Company class; representatives of Karl Strauss Brewing Co. and Luce Forward, second- and third-place winners respectively, Large Company class; Bill Trumpfheller, Nuffer, Smith, Tucker, Inc., third-place winner, Small Company class; Don Teemsma, Ideal Plumbing, Heating, Air & Electrical, second-place winner, Small Company class; and Reo Carr, vice president, editor-in-chief, *San Diego Business Journal.*

Qualcomm. Company awards were presented in several categories.

In the Small Company category, the award was presented to Crystal Pyramid Productions. Don Teemsma of Ideal Plumbing, Heating, Air & Electrical and Bill Trumpfheller of Nuffer, Smith, Tucker, Inc. received second- and third-place awards.

The Medium Company award was presented to Bill Howe Plumbing. ESET North America and Bruce Knowlton of Moss Adams, LLP received second- and third-place awards.

In the Large Company category, Frank Urtasun accepted the Heilbron Award for SDG&E. Chris Cramer's Karl Strauss Brewing Company and Bill Earley's Luce Forward won second and third place, respectively.

In addition to about 200 members, 150 guests also attended the very special meeting.

New Badges and Centennial Logo

For the first time in seventy-one years, the Rotary name badges were redesigned, the work done by Schwartz Design Group, Inc. In addition, a new logo was designed, reflecting the one-hundred-year history of Club 33.

Timeline

January 12, 2010 – Disaster in Haiti, where an earthquake registered at 7.0. Early death toll estimated to be over 150,000. On the first anniversary of the earthquake, January 12, 2011, Haitian Prime Minister Jean-Max Bellerive said the death toll from the quake was more than 316,000, raising the figures from previous estimates.

October 12, 2010 – Thirty-three Chilean miners are rescued from a mine after being trapped underground for sixty-nine days without casualties.

March 11–12, 2011 – In Japan, an earthquake registered at 9.0 and tsunami caused devastation. According to official estimates, 15,848 people died in the tragedy and another 3,305 people are recorded as missing.

CHAPTER ELEVEN

The Centennial Celebration

2011

> *One Hundred Years and Counting...*
> *The next one hundred years—a tradition of*
> *leadership, fellowship, and service above self.*

▲**PLANNING FOR THE CENTENNIAL YEAR OF THE SAN DIEGO ROTARY OFFICIALLY BEGAN** when President Hartman announced at the February 26, 2009 club meeting that longtime Rotarian Ben Clay (president, 1989–1990) accepted Hartman's "call" to chair the yearlong Centennial Celebration. Clay wisely called upon several members of Club 33 to take on specific projects. In addition to Clay and Vice Chair Sandy Mayberry, other energetic members were Mike Caruso, Bink Cook, Pat Crowell, Debbie Day, Tom Gable, Tom Gehring, Joyce Glazer, Wayne Goodermote, Stan Hartman, Pauline Hill, Jo Dee Jacob, Chet Lathrop, Kimberly Layton, Jill Spitzer, David Oates, Steve Porter, Patti Roscoe, Bonnie Schwartz, Dick Troncone, Mark Trotter, and Irene Wells.

Part of the planning process included ongoing discussions regarding the goals—both external and internal—of Club 33's Centennial Celebration. The external focus would be to bring attention to Rotary and in the process attract new members. It was also decided that there was no need to reinvent the wheel, but to use existing events in the San Diego area to partner in the Centennial Celebration. The internal focus would be to promote pride in the club and to educate, motivate, and participate.

Tux & Tennies

The first of a series of community events was the San Diego Symphony's annual "Tux & Tennies" Summer Pops Kick-off. Chaired by Joyce Glazer, other committee members included Steve Bond, Sandi Cottrell, Richard Cox, Paul Hartley III, Stan Hartman, Kevin Leap, Jen Martino, and David Oates. During the evening, Club 33 presented a $20,000 check in honor of the Symphony's just-completed yearlong centennial celebration.

Happy Birthday to Club 33!

The official birthday of Club 33 was celebrated at the Founders Day meeting on November 3, 2011. Chaired by past president Mark Trotter, the committee included Mark Allan, Bink Cook, Pat Crowell, Chris Elliott, Tom Karlo, Steve Porter, Patti Roscoe, and Jean Young.

The La Jolla Brass entertained and played, among other tunes, "Alexander's Ragtime Band," the number-one hit of 1911, the year of Club 33's founding. Chair of the Day Ben Clay spoke eloquently of the many accomplishments made during the club's one hundred years in San Diego. District Governor Larry Sundram presented a special award from Rotary International. Mayor Jerry Sanders presented a proclamation from the City of San Diego, and resolutions were received from Toni Atkinson, the 76th Congressional District, and from Christine Kehoe, the 39th Senatorial District. In

addition, former governor Pete Wilson sent his congratulations. Twenty-seven past presidents were in attendance and stood for well-deserved applause. The members of the Bequest Society were also recognized for their contributions.

A stunning centennial video was narrated by Mark Trotter and many "descendents" of Club 33 were also recognized, including the Frosts, Fletchers, Jessops, and others honoring the legacies of their parents, grandparents, and great-grandparents.

The Club 33 Singers celebrated the May 4, 1987 date that brought women into the club with their own rendition of "There is Nothin' Like a Dame." Natasha Josefowitz entertained with her special poetry. She and her late husband, Herman Gadon, were the club's "first couple."

◢ A large crowd of Rotarians and guests attended the one-hundredth-birthday luncheon for Club 33.

Bill Earley represented newer members of the club and spoke of those who encouraged him along the way, including RI Trustee Steve Brown, Judge Al Harutunian III, and Tyler Cramer. The Club 33 Singers sang "You Gotta Have Heart," and a champagne toast and rousing "Happy Birthday" sung by the audience ended a truly magnificent meeting.

Additional Centennial Events

More events were on tap which would close out the yearlong celebration, including the annual Rotarians at Work Day chaired by Robert Borgman on April 29, 2012; Jack-in-the-Box Hoops at the Beach on May 19–20, 2012; and lastly, the presentation of the Heilbron Awards, chaired by Bonnie Schwartz and Karen Hutchens, which took place at the June 7, 2012 meeting.

LOOKING AHEAD: THE NEXT THREE PRESIDENTS, WAYNE, JO DEE, AND CHUCK

A major component of Club 33's success is the vision that connects the presidents from term to term and keeps Club 33 members focused on significant goals while allowing for a unique presidential personality to shine through for each term. These efforts result in an engaged membership

Holiday Bowl Parade, December 28, 2011

Approximately fifty members of Club 33 and members of the Jackie Robinson YMCA participated in the Holiday Bowl Parade. Chaired by Michelle Candland, the float was created by Charlie Trembler's Big Events, Inc., with inspiration from Centennial Chair Ben Clay.

▲ We love a parade! Celebrating the Holiday Bowl at the parade in downtown San Diego.

▲ The Rotary Balloon was a big hit at the Holiday Bowl Parade.

Salute to the Military, February 9

On February 9, the club's annual Salute to the Military luncheon, chaired by David Oates, was celebrated with a special centennial flare.

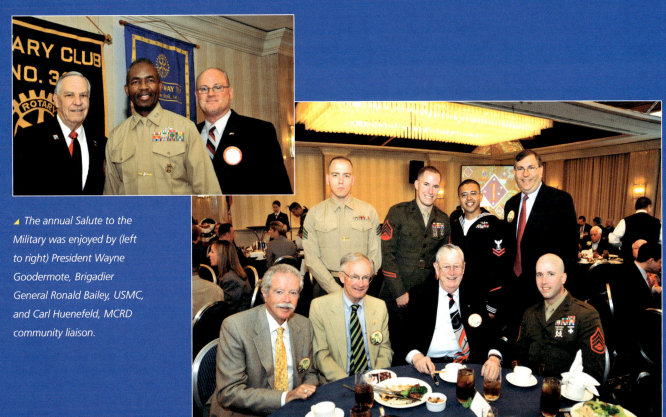

▲ The annual Salute to the Military was enjoyed by (left to right) President Wayne Goodermote, Brigadier General Ronald Bailey, USMC, and Carl Huenefeld, MCRD community liaison.

▲ Seated (from left): John Rebelo, Chip Goodwin, and Pat Crowell; standing (far right): Al Harutunian III.

and projects that continue to reflect "Service Above Self."

In 2008, a formal process was started by President Stan Hartman with regularly scheduled meetings of the past president, current president, and president-elect with the executive director to review goals, projects, and progress along with membership and programs. During this—the all-important centennial year—the troika of Schwartz, Goodermote, and Jacob met regularly.

PRESIDENT WAYNE GOODERMOTE
July 1, 2011 – June 30, 2012

"I joined Rotary to pay back; it's a hook to get people to do more."

President Goodermote's theme for his term is "Enjoying Rotary While Celebrating Our Centennial Year." He adopted the well-known equation "$E=MC^2$" to one where "E is for Enjoyment in Rotary, M is for Member, and C is for Commitment." That translates into "For every bit of commitment by the member to Rotary, the enjoyment goes up exponentially."

Goodermote's vision is focused on three areas. The first is increasing membership, the "M" in the equation, with special emphasis on recruiting of women, younger members, and expanding the ethnic representation within Club 33. The second and third areas focus on the "C", commitment to philanthropic and mission support. He used the Centennial Celebration as an opportunity for members to "gift" to the club in order to help secure its financial health for the next one hundred years. He encouraged members to take advantage of the meaningful opportunities to serve by actively participating on one or more of the fifty-seven committees. As a commitment during the centennial year, the "100 Minutes Program" was initiated with Goodermote challenging every Rotarian to spend at least one hundred minutes each quarter volunteering, whether reading to a student, taking a senior to an appointment, or selecting from the hundreds of other ways to help.

PRESIDENT JO DEE C. JACOB
July 1, 2012 – June 30, 2013

"Make new friends, but keep the old."

Jo Dee Jacob, the chief executive officer of the Girl Scouts of San Diego, will be the first not-for-profit executive to serve as president of Club 33. Her areas of concentration emphasize the sustainability of the club through membership, philanthropy, and growth. Financial strength would be achieved through planned

giving (the Bequest Society) and appropriate recognition of major donors. She will continue to seek young and multi-generational new members whose diversity reflects the community, and to focus on vibrant weekly meetings to keep members engaged and committed to Club 33.

Jacob also spoke of the need to examine future trends, such as the consolidation of clubs where appropriate. "We must be strong and right-sized." She stated the need to continue to use modern forms of technology as new ways to do business, and to carefully look at opportunities to build on partnerships and alliances within the community.

PRESIDENT CHUCK PRETTO
July 1, 2013 – June 30, 2014

"Rotary is the love of my life after my family."

Chuck Pretto joined Club 33 in 1992 and credits past president Jim Hughes for deepening his involvement in Rotary through the Youth Exchange Committee. Ultimately, he and his family hosted a foreign student, and everyone in his family was hooked from then on.

Pretto's goals for his presidency include youth-oriented projects, especially Camp Enterprise, Interact committees, and the Rotaract Committee; highlighting partnerships with not-for-profit and other community organizations; and continuing emphasis on fellowship among members. Pretto, who loves to cook, stated that he plans to host dinner parties for groups of members in his home. He referred to the committees as the real gems of Rotary, which must have the support of members. "I need to be a strong cheerleader for those committees."

The Legacy Continues

The financial health of Club 33 depends on growing membership and through the years, a great way to advance the cause of Rotary has been through a multi-generational membership. Descendents of original members come from the Heilbron, Hazzard, Brockett, Goodwin, Kelsey, and Kettner families, among others. More recently, names such as Frost, Jessop, Nestor, Hartley, and Morton were added to the legacy list.

Jo Abbey Briggs joined in 1996, and her daughter, Kimberly Layton, joined in 2001. Dodie Rotherham (1988) was joined by her son Jim Rotherham in 1994. The first father-daughter combo was Rod Eales (1976) and Shandon Harbour (2008). William Enright joined in 1970, and his son, Kevin, joined in 1997. The first official "couple" was Natasha Josefowitz, who joined in 1987 (one of the first women to join), and her late husband, Herman Gadon, who joined in 1990. The second couple was Ben (1978) and Nickki Clay (1991).

More recently, "couple" members include Linda (2002) and Terry (1989) Moore; Judy Thompson (2007) and Michael Conner (2009); Karen (2008) and Andy (2002) Hewitt; Sharon (1992) and Carl (1977) Hilliard; Diane (1998) and Roy (1997) Bell; Linda (2001) and Larry (2007) Stirling; and Jan (1997) and John (2002) Driscoll.

THE NEXT ONE HUNDRED YEARS

As the club leadership considers the direction for the next one hundred years,

emphasis will continue to be on member efforts to improve not just San Diego, but the world through community, vocational, international, and new generations service. Each year, three goals must be achieved: to attract and retain new members; to promote philanthropy; and to create opportunities for member involvement and participation. In each of the Avenues of Service, there are key initiatives. Club 33 will reach its goals when each member takes ownership of a goal and a key initiative.

By the end of the first decade of the twenty-first century, Club 33 was contributing upwards of $200,000 annually to local, national, and international charitable missions. Committee members were providing more than 9,000 hours of community service and supporting 8,000 individuals in need. The key element continues to be an amazing membership that embraces a tradition of leadership, fellowship, and service above self. May that continue into the next century of service!

As Bill Earley said at the one-hundredth-birthday celebration on November 4, 2011, "Don't wait, participate!"

Here's to the next one hundred years for Club 33!

In Memoriam

Bruce N. Moore

Hugh C. Carter

Charles W. Christensen

Joseph P. Flynn

David Detrick

Rotary's One Hundred Years of Quiet Service to San Diego

(The following letter to the editor by Wayne Goodermote and Bonnie Schwartz appeared in the November 4, 2011 edition of the San Diego Union Tribune. *Goodermote is president of Club 33 and Schwartz is immediate past president.)*

What began a century ago this week when 11 San Diego businessmen met over lunch at the 1-year-old U.S. Grant Hotel to launch Rotary Club 33 has grown to become one of the five largest clubs in the world with almost 550 members. Along the way to its centennial celebration this month, Club 33 has exemplified the concept of what service clubs aim to achieve.

The goals are to bring together business and professional leaders to provide humanitarian service, encourage high ethical standards in all vocations, and help build goodwill and peace in the world. In that role, Club 33 has contributed, often quietly and behind the scenes, to actively supporting important causes, from local military, medical, environmental and educational programs to providing humanitarian assistance throughout the world.

It's a record few people are aware of. The tally reaches into the millions of dollars and hundreds of thousands of hours contributed under the theme of "service above self." Highlights over its 100-year history include:

- Club 33's first public service project was the contribution of materials for the Broadway Pier in 1912; its first youth program launched Big Brothers in 1913.
- Thereafter, the club extended its youth work to aiding orphans, needy families, and crippled children, and in 1917 it sponsored creation of the San Diego Area Boy Scout Council. In ensuing decades its work expanded to support Girl Scouts and create Boys & Girls Clubs.
- Club 33 has renovated gardens in Balboa Park, made a major contribution toward creation of the Burn Center at UCSD Medical Center, and supported cultural, educational, charity and historic preservation projects.
- It helped found Monarch School, the groundbreaking educational institution in San Diego for homeless and other children at risk.
- It financed a park along the Trolley tracks by Seaport Village to turn a blighted area into a popular path for San Diegans and visitors alike.
- Club 33 sends a surgical team from Mercy Hospital and volunteers to impoverished parts of Mexico each year to perform surgeries on children with cleft palates and other deformities so they have a chance for future happiness in life.
- Volunteers build houses, school rooms and sanitation facilities in Tijuana and other border cities.

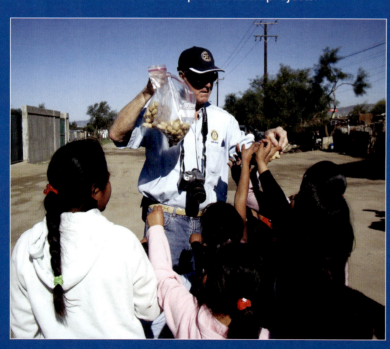

▲ *Bob Fletcher hands out treats to the youngsters on the annual Fish Across the Border trip to Mexico.*

▲ *Steve Oggel, Mike Caruso, Bill Dick, Kevin Clark, Sally King, and Hank Killmar host traveling members of our military forces at the USO lounge at La Jolla at Christmas.*

- ▲ Club 33 conducts an annual Camp Enterprise to introduce high school juniors to business, marketing, capitalism and entrepreneurship.
- ▲ From a single Club 33 in 1911, Rotary has grown to 62 clubs in San Diego with more than 3,400 members contributing to the community.
- ▲ Rotary Club 33 also contributes to the global program to eradicate polio as part of the worldwide organization of more than 1.2 million business, professional and community members in 33,000 Rotary clubs throughout the world.

Civic organizations are often joked about as being just clubs for lunching and networking. The opportunity for fellowship over food is surely part of the tradition, but Club 33 has elevated the art. Its meetings serve as a popular venue for high-profile speakers, which have included former President George H.W. Bush, former British Prime Minister Margaret Thatcher, T. Boone Pickens, Kyoto Prize laureates, university presidents, heads of San Diego's most innovative and successful organizations, political and governmental leaders, economists, foreign dignitaries, and many best-selling authors and renowned artists.

Club leadership has included famous local names (Spreckels, Fletcher, Marston, Kettner, Price, Luce and Jessop) and the business leaders of San Diego, plus mayors, councilmen, county supervisors, state and national legislators, judges and commissioners, and heads of most community-oriented organizations, professional societies, and business associations at local, state and national levels.

With its first 100 years now behind it, the "Downtown Club" has far exceeded its geographic reach. It is committed to continuing its tradition of supporting San Diego causes while pursuing new frontiers for contributing in the areas of community, vocational and international service.

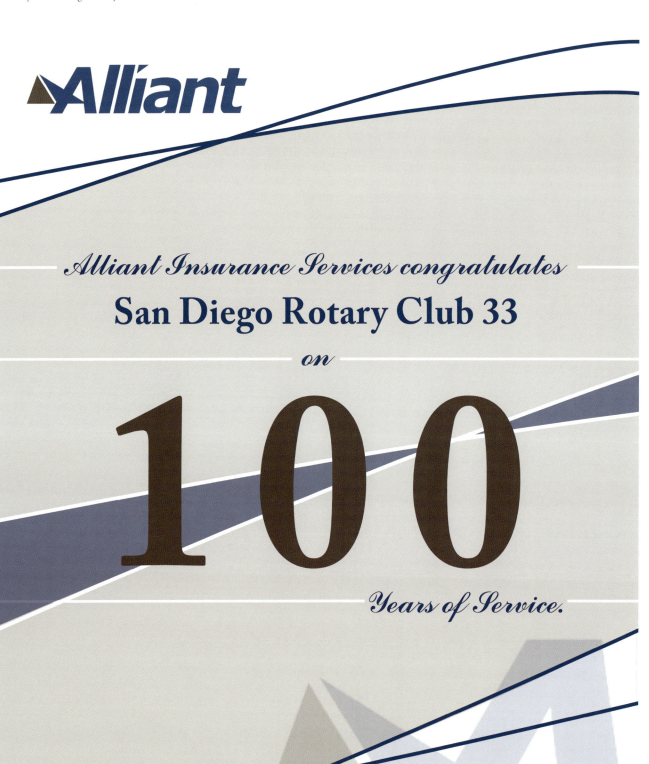

San Diego Rotary Club 33
BEQUEST SOCIETY

Anonymous
Mark Allan
John Alioto
Kenneth W. Andersen
Jack Anthony
Warren J. Arnett, Jr.
Frank V. Arrington
Marten Barry, Jr.
Philip C. Blair
Rudi M. Brewster
Michelle Candland
Ellen Casey
Chris Christopher
Benjamin G. & Nicole A. Clay
Michael Conner
Mary Colacicco
Barbara Cook
Richard D. Coutts, M.D.
Joseph W. Craver
Frederick P. Crowell
Stephen P. Cushman
Jack E. Damson
Richard A. DeBolt
Jeremiah Doran
Craig S. Evanco
Daryl E. Ferguson
Joan Friedenberg
G. T. Frost, Jr.
Frederick A. Frye, M.D.
Kathryn Fulhorst
George Lewis Gildred
Wayne K. Goodermote
Stanford F. Hartman, Jr.
James C. Haugh
Andrew & Karen Hewitt
Ann Hill
Stephen Hubbard
James M. Hughes

Bruce A. Hunt
Karen Hutchens
Jo Dee C. Jacob
George Carter Jessop
James C. Jessop
Larry Kuntz
Robert C. Kyle
Sarah K. Lamade
Guy Maddox
William C. McDade, M.D.
Lisa S. Miller, M.D.
John L. Morrell
Greg Noonan
Kay North
John Ohanian
Joanne Pastula
Betty Peabody
Charles J. Pretto
John G. Rebelo, Jr.
Arthur L. Rivkin
Patricia L. Roscoe
Norbert Sanders
Bonnie Schwartz
Nancy Scott
Larry G. Showley
Suzanne Spafford
Lawrence Stirling
Linda Stirling
Donald V. Tartre
Judy Thompson
Mark C. Trotter
Thomas R. Vecchione, M.D.
Bert E. Wahlen
Geri Ann Warnke
Karin Winner
Jean Young
Greg Zinser

In Memory of Lowell Davies
By Darlene Gould Davies

- Mr. San Diego, 1979
- Secretary to E. W. Scripps
- J.D., U. C. Berkeley, Boalt Hall School of Law
- Phi Beta Kappa
- Appointed & reappointed to Advisory Committee for the National Endowment for the Arts by Presidents Eisenhower and Kennedy
- Appointed by Governor Reagan to California Arts Commission for 8 years; Chair, 1 year
- President and Chair of the Old Globe Theater Board of Directors for more than three decades
- The Old Globe Lowell Davies Festival Theater announced in 1983 and officially opened in 1985
- Included among "50 Most Influential People of the Last 50 Years" in *San Diego Magazine*, October 1998
- His eulogy delivered in United States Congress, 1983

Photo by James Milch

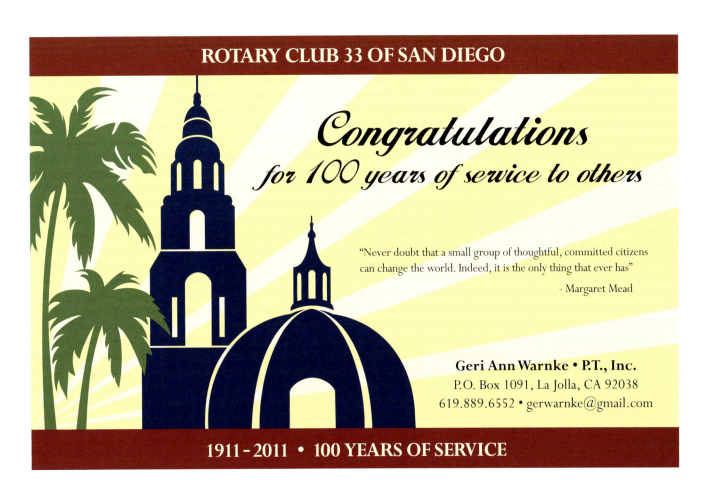

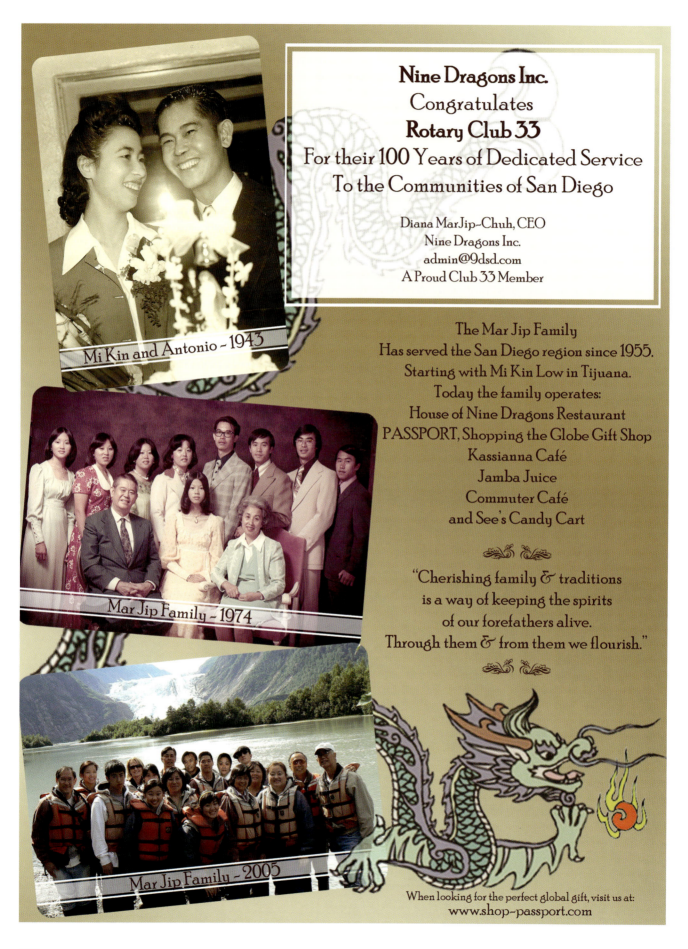

Mi Kin and Antonio ~ 1943

Mar Jip Family ~ 1974

Mar Jip Family ~ 2005

Celebrating 100 years of Rotary
100 years of Girl Scouts
100 years of leadership

Sharing common values of service above self.
Building future leaders for our club, community, nation and the world.

Yesterday's Girl Scouts...today's Rotarians

Diane Bell	Daryl Day	Jo Dee C. Jacob	Holly Pobst
Kimberly Bond	Martha Dennis	Divya Kakaiya	Jenni Prisk
Lisa Bruner	Solveig Deuprey	Katherine Kennedy	Susan Rehm
Barbara Bry	Jan Driscoll	Sarah Lamade	Patti Roscoe
Michelle Candland	Bonnie Dumanis	Yvonne Larsen	Donita Rotherham
Ellen Casey	Margaret Eddy	Kimberley Layton	Deborah Ruane
Nicole Clay	Christina Elliott	Cathleen LeClair	Angela Salinas
Barbara Cook	Judy Forrester	Leane Marchese	Bonnie Schwartz
Paula Cordeiro	Joan Friedenberg	Jennifer Martino	Nancy Scott
Darlene Davies	Kathryn Fulhorst	Carolyn McCormick	Susan Snow
Janie Davis	Sally Furay	Judith McDonald	Suzanne Spafford
	Joy Hamer	M. Margaret McKeown	Roberta Spoon
	Shandon Harbour	Jackie Meyer	Linda Stirling
	Karen Hewitt	Kris Michell	Carol Summerhays
	Ann Hill	Lisa Miller	Judy Thompson
	Sharon Hilliard	Linda Moore	Rebecca Tuggle
	Pamela Holden	Patricia Moore	Geri Ann Warnke
	Marie Huff	Kay North	Irene Wells
	Karen Hutchens	Claudia Obertreis	Betty Jo Williams
		Kathleen Pacurar	Cheryl Wilson
		Joanne Pastula	Karin Winner
		Kathleen Pasulka-Brown	Jean Young
		Betty Peabody	Charlene Zettel
			Mary Zoeller

Girl Scout Margaret McKeown (1968) successfully litigated for women in Rotary (1986-87). Today, she serves as U.S. Circuit Judge, U.S. Court of Appeals (9th Circuit).

girl scouts
1912-2012

THANK YOU TO ALL THE MEMBERS WHO HELPED MAKE THIS HISTORY BOOK POSSIBLE BY ADVERTISING. HAPPY CENTENNIAL!

Congratulations to
The Rotary Club of San Diego
For 100 Years of Service to
San Diego and the World

Jim, Carmen & Karen Sofia Hughes

2247 San Diego Avenue, Suite 236, San Diego, CA 92110

Dear Dad,

Among my fondest childhood memories is attending Rotary with you from an early age.

Now I am proud to serve with you as a member of San Diego Rotary 33.

Thank you for passing on the Rotary tradition.

Paul Nestor

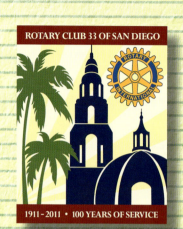

SCHWARTZ**D**ESIGN**G**ROUP

BRANDING • ADVERTISING • IDENTITIES/LOGOS • WEBSITES

MORONGO BAND OF MISSION INDIANS

A SOVEREIGN NATION

LOGO, INVITATION & PACKAGING WITH A "WOW" FACTOR

Morongo Band of Mission Indians

DISTINCTIVE LOGOS

EFFECTIVE BRANDING

Myriad Software: Print ad campaigns, website, banner ads, brochures, eAds. (since 2001)

MEMORABLE MARKETING

West Laurel Hill Cemetery: 224 page coffee table book, print ad campaigns, style guide, app design, brochures, event theme identities.

WEB PLANNING & DESIGN

Young + Co., a commercial interior design firm.

Hutchens PR

DISTINCTIVE LOGO, STATIONERY SUITE & WEBSITE

Hutchens PR

BRANDING FOR NON-PROFITS

Country Friends: Major fundraiser fashion show direct mail invitation materials.

RESULTS ORIENTED ADVERTISING & WEB DESIGN

Jessop's Jeweler. (Since 1987)

CONSISTENT BRANDING

Robbins Geller: "The Future of Corporate reform" conference logo & all marketing materials. (since 2001)

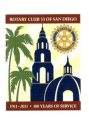

CELEBRATING ROTARY CLUB 33 OF SAN DIEGO'S 100th ANNIVERSARY

Event logo, badges, banners, posters commemmorating Rotary's service to the community.

www.schwartzdesigngroup.com • 619 291 8878 • Since 1972

sdasecurity.com

Established 1930

CONGRATULATIONS CLUB 33

*on 100 years of service
to San Diego.*

Safety. Security. *Service.*

SDA Security salutes Rotary Club 33 for one hundred years of dedicated service to San Diego. As a proud, proactive Club 33 member since 1976, we look forward to continuing our commitment to Rotary for many, many years to come.

Supporting and Protecting San Diego Since 1930

Delivering meaningful service to both our community and our customers defines the culture of commitment that has driven SDA Security for over 80 years.

In that time, we've worked tirelessly to emulate the "Service Above Self" ethos that defines Rotary Club 33's commitment to excellence.

A Commitment to Community

We're committed to bettering the lives of San Diegans through our involvement with organizations making a positive impact on our local communities and the larger world.

A Commitment to Quality

The SDA team is driven to deliver the highest quality service to our community and customers while creating a positive work environment for our employees to grow and flourish.

A Commitment to the Future

We're proud of our long history of dedication to serving the needs of San Diego's homeowners, businesses and government organizations. As San Diego's partner in protection, we look forward to embracing this commitment to quality and community as we evolve and grow.

Join the conversation:

CA License #245668 | ACO #046

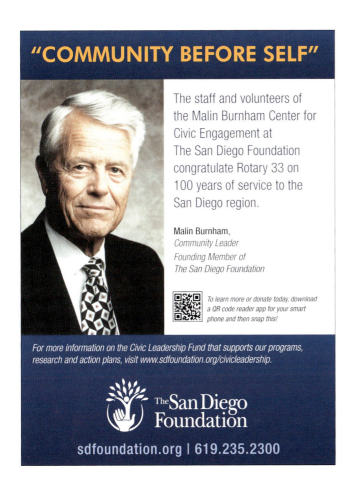

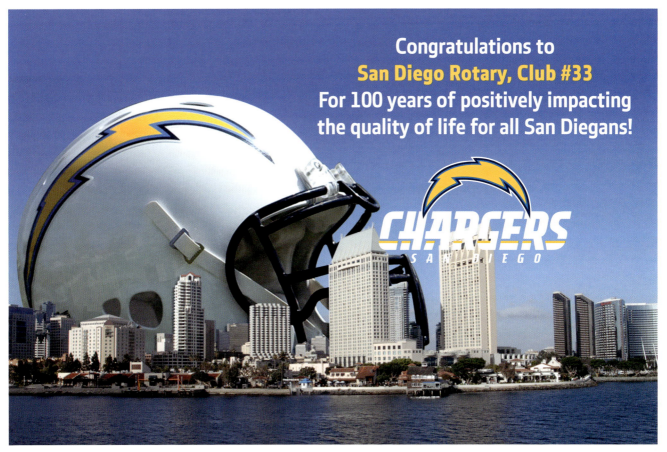

THE *energy* OF
service

SDG&E® salutes *San Diego Rotary Club 33* for fostering the solid principles that are shaping the leaders of tomorrow. We believe integrity, responsibility and service to others are the cornerstones of a great community and a great nation. And we're proud to help support organizations dedicated to the positive ideals that make a notable difference for all of us. We're committed to being an active partner and contributor to the local community.

Congratulations on reaching the remarkable milestone of 100 years of service.

sdge.com

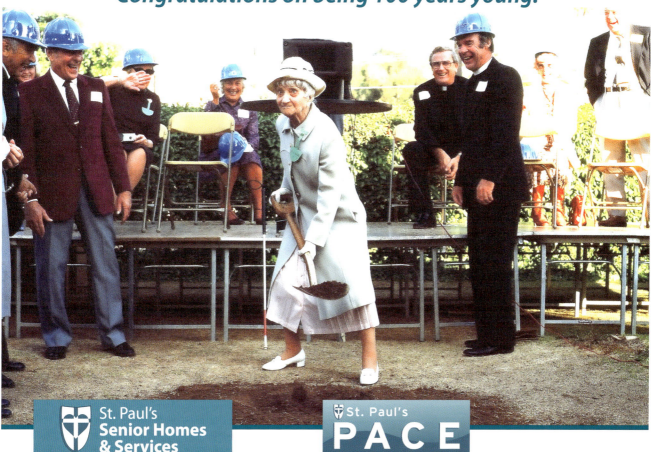

Legendary

The physicians of Sharp Rees-Stealy Medical Group congratulate Rotary Club 33 of San Diego on 100 years of service to San Diego.

Since 1923 we, too, have been caring for the community. Our longstanding commitment continues with the new Sharp Rees-Stealy Medical Center Downtown, opening summer 2012.

Paul Harris Fellows

Dominick Addario, MD
Vernon V. Aguirre
John R. Ahlering, MD
George D. Alexander
John Alioto
Mark B. Allan
Kenneth W. Andersen
John A. Anewalt
John R. Anthony, OD
Douglas Arbon, MD
Warren J. Arnett, Jr.
Robert W. Arnhym
Frank V. Arrington
Greg Augustine
Donald C. Balfour, MD
Walter R. Barrett
Marten Barry, Jr.
Richard C. Baxter
William E. Beamer
Dudley A. Beckett
Diane C. Bell
Roy Morrow Bell
Amnon Ben-Yehuda
Jack M. Berkman
Philip C. Blair
Charles B. Blake
Craig Blower
Peter W. Bowie
Rudi M. Brewster
Sheldon I. Brockett, DDS
Daniel P. Brogan
Carl R. Brown
Gerard J. Brown
James S. Brown
Michael W. Brunker
James H. Buley
Dennis Burks
Lyle W. Butler
Robert E. Cairncross
Steven E. Cairncross
Ian D. Campbell

Michelle Candland
Jack A. Carpenter
Samuel Carpenter
Reid H. Carr
Robert A. Carroll
Ellen M. Casey
Patrick W. Caughey
Karen Cebreros
Edward R. Chaplin, MD
Charles H. Christian
Chris A. Christopher, Jr.
Vincent R. Ciruzzi
Larry R. Clapper
Garet B. Clark
Kevin Clark
Benjamin G. Clay
Nicole A. Clay
Robert K. Cleator, Jr.
Mary G. Colacicco, PhD
Cynthia M. Coleman
H. Michael Collins
Michael J. Conner
Barbara Cook
Paula A. Cordeiro
Richard D. Coutts, MD
Christopher Cramer
Tyler W. Cramer
Joseph W. Craver
Linda Crogan
Dean M. Crowder
Frederick P. Crowell
Phillip L. Currie
Lawrence M. Cushman
Stephen P. Cushman
Jose G. da Rosa
Jack E. Damson
Michael G. Daniels
Darlene G. Davies
Richard H. Davis
Daryl E. Day
Thomas B. Day, PhD

Richard A. DeBolt
Arthur DeFever
Martha G. Dennis, PhD
Robert D. Dicioccio
William L. Dick
Jeremiah Doran
Rodger W. Dougherty
Jan S. Driscoll
George F. Driver
Charles W. Duddles
Peter L. Duncan
Berit N. Durler
Rodney R. Eales
Margaret F. Eddy
Marlee J. Ehrenfeld
Raymond G. Ellis
Peter K. Ellsworth
Matthew Engel
Craig S. Evanco
Joseph N. Farrage
Daryl E. Ferguson
Thompson Fetter
Andrew Fichthorn
James Fitzpatrick
Robert C. Fletcher
C. F. Flynn
Howard B. Frank
Joan Friedenberg
Bruce H. Frost
Gordon T. Frost, Jr.
Frederick A. Frye, MD
Kathryn Fulhorst
James R. Furby
Tom Gable
Joyce M. Gattas
Tom Gehring
George Lewis Gildred
Philip L. Gildred, Jr.
Ian M. Gill
Edwin L. Glazener, MD
Joyce A. Glazer

James R. Goode
Wayne K. Goodermote
Ewart W. Goodwin, Jr.
Douglas B. Gordon
William D. Gore
Gary G. Gould
Richard M. Green, DPM
Richard B. Gulley
Vance A. Gustafson
Roger W. Haines, Jr.
James M. Hall
Shandon Harbour
George B. Harris III
Paul J. Hartley III
Stanford F. Hartman, Jr.
Albert T. Harutunian III
John S. Hattox, MD
James C. Haugh
John S. Hawkins
William E. Hendrix, DDS
Daniel D. Herde
William M. Herrin,
    USMC (Ret.)
Andrew W. Hewitt
Pauline H. Hill
Carl B. Hilliard, Jr.
Sharon E. Hilliard
John H. Hinrichs
Larry Hoeksema
Joseph M. Horiye
Robert B. Horsman
Elizabeth M. Hubbard
J. Stephen Hubbard
Marie K. Huff
James M. Hughes
Darrell Hunsaker
Bruce A. Hunt
Howard Hunt
Karen Hutchens
Robert W. Hymes, DDS
David W. Jackson

James H. Jackson, Jr., PhD
Kirk I. Jackson
Richard W. Jackson
Jo Dee C. Jacob
J. Robert Jacobs, MD
George C. Jessop
Gerald C. Jessop
James C. Jessop
Claudia A. Johnson
R. Bruce Johnson, MD
Michael B. Jones
R. Kendal Jones
Morton C. Jorgensen, MD
Natasha Josefowitz, PhD
Mel I. Katz
Edward T. Keating
Robert A. Kelly
Katherine Kennedy
Michael Kenny
Donald B. Kent
James G. Kidrick
Henry M. Killmar
Ray King
Russell W. Kirbey
Philip M. Klauber
Bill Kolender
Larry Kuntz
Richard Kwiatkowski
Robert C. Kyle
Walter Lam
Sarah K. Lamade
Roy E. Lange
Thomas F. Larwin
Chester A. Lathrop
Nancy S. Laturno-Bojanic
Kimberley B. Layton
Cathleen LeClair
John W. Ledford
Richard S. Ledford
John R. Lindholm, MD
Lewis M. Linson
Andrew J. Liska
John Littrell
Gordon K. Lutes
Guy Maddox
Sandra L. Mayberry
Sandra L. McBrayer

Scott McClendon
Carolyn B. McCormick
William C. McDade, MD
Judith E. McDonald
Rick McElvain
Keith McKenzie
William M. McKenzie, Jr.
Ray McKewon
Daniel G. McKinney
Ailene McManus
Michael Meaney
Laurence A. Miller, MD
Lisa S. Miller, MD
Emile Misiraca
Linda Moore
Terry Moore
John L. Morrell
Michael A. Morton
Thomas F. Mosher, MD
Vincent E. Mudd
Steven J. Mueller
Edward C. Muns
Michael A. Murphy
Mike W. Murphy
Douglas G. Myers
Robert C. Myers
Edward J. Nares
Vincent Nares
Gary R. Nelson
Mark Nelson
Burton H. Nestor
Paul Nestor
William W. Newbern
Charles E. Nickel
James R. Nickel, MD
Gregory V. Noonan
Kay G. North
David B. Oates
Claudia Obertreis
Stephen P. Oggel
Frank Panarisi
Leon W. Parma
Joanne Pastula
Kathleen A. Pasulka-Brown
Douglas C. Paul
Frank Pavel, DDS

VAdm. R. E. Peet,
   USN (Ret.)
Gloria Penner
H. Newton Pollock
Michael B. Poynor
Charles J. Pretto
H. P. Purdon
Ross M. Pyle
Donald G. Ramras, MD
Victor G. Ramsauer
John G. Rebelo, Jr.
Susan J. Rehm
John K. Reid
James O. Reynolds
Lawrence Richman
Garry Ridge
Samuel M. Rinaker, Jr.
Arthur L. Rivkin
Patricia L. Roscoe
Donita Rotherham
Michael S. Rowan
Eugene W. Rumsey, Jr., MD
Robert G. Russell, Jr.
Harold G. Sadler
Norbert Sanders
Eugene H. Sapper
G. Bradford Saunders
Douglas F. Sawyer
Donald L. Schoell
Bonnie Schwartz
Nancy Scott
Larry G. Showley
Alvin J. Sibel
Christopher J. Sichel
L. Clark Siebrand
Scott H. Silverman
Sidney R. Silverman
Michael J. Sise, MD
Sidney C. Smith, Jr., MD
Susan Snow
Suzanne Spafford
Roberta J. Spoon
Craig A. Starkey
Harold B. Starkey, Jr.
Claudio Stemberger
Cecil H. Steppe
Lawrence Stirling

Linda Stirling
John D. Sullivan
Richard M. Sullivan, MD
Marc Tarasuck
Donald V. Tartre
Paul K. Tchang
Donald Teemsma, Jr.
M. Murray Tenney, Jr.
Robert C. Thaxton, Jr.
William R. Thaxton
Judy Thompson
Stephen F. Treadgold
Albert E. Trepte
Richard A. Troncone
Mark C. Trotter
Jerald Van Ert
Paul Van Roon
Denis K. Vanier
Thomas R. Vecchione, MD
Bert E. Wahlen
Ramona Walker
Richard C. Walker
Mary L. Walshok
Geri Ann Warnke
Allan Wasserman
Louis M. Wax
Irene J. Wells
Jack K. White
Colin W. Wied
Cheryl Wilson
Douglas Wilson
Thomas D. Wilson
Karin E. Winner
Jere L. With
Robert M. Witty
Jean Young
Joseph A. Zakowski, DDS
Paul E. Zeigler, DDS
Greg Zinser
John J. Zygowicz

Donors and Club 33 Fellows

* Deceased

THE THOMAS W. SEFTON SOCIETY
$1,000,000+

Thomas W. Sefton*

THE ROTARY GEARWHEEL SOCIETY
$500,000-999,999

THE ROTARY COGS SOCIETY
$250,000-499,999

THE JAMES M. HUGHES SOCIETY
$100,000-249,999

James M. Hughes

THE WILLIAM T. WARD SOCIETY
$50,000-99,999

William T. Ward*

THE JOHN T. MARTIN SOCIETY
$25,000-49,999

Amnon Ben-Yehuda
John T. Martin*

COMMUNITY PARTNER
$10,000-24,999

Frank V. Arrington
Roy M. Bell
Michelle Candland
Paula A. Cordeiro
Peter L. Duncan
Henry Garnjobst, Jr.*
George L. Gildred
Wayne K. Goodermote
John S. Hawkins
Robert B. Horsman
Kirk I. Jackson

Philip M. Klauber
John L. Morrell
Patricia L. Roscoe
Deborah Szekely
Diana D. Venable*
Geri Ann Warnke
Jack K. White

PRESIDENT'S CIRCLE
$5,000-9,999

John R. Ahlering, MD
Rudi M. Brewster
Ian D. Campbell
Ellen M. Casey
Benjamin G. Clay
Barbara Cook
Richard H. Davis
George F. Driver
Robert C. Fletcher
Gary G. Gould
James W. Groen
Paul J. Hartley III
Stanford F. Hartman, Jr.
David W. Jackson
Jo Dee C. Jacob
Oliver B. James, Jr.*
William C. McDade, MD
Daniel G. McKinney
James F. Mulvaney*
Frank L. Pavel, Jr., DMD
VAdm. R. E. Peet,
   USN (Ret.)
Charles J. Pretto
H. P. Purdon
Robert G. Russell, Jr.
Bonnie Schwartz
Alvin J. Sibel
Lawrence Stirling
Linda Stirling
Richard A. Troncone
Thomas R. Vecchione, MD

SURVIVING CLUB 33 FOUNDING FELLOWS

Frederick A. Frye, MD
George C. Jessop
Philip M. Klauber
Nancy Scott
Harold B. Starkey, Jr.
Geri Ann Warnke

CURRENT CLUB 33 FELLOWS

Dominick Addario, MD
John R. Ahlering, MD
George D. Alexander
John Alioto
Mark B. Allan
Kenneth W. Andersen
John R. Anthony, OD
Warren J. Arnett, Jr.
Robert W. Arnhym
Greg Augustine
Donald C. Balfour, MD
Walter R. Barrett
Marten Barry, Jr.
William E. Beamer
Dudley A. Beckett
Jack M. Berkman
Philip C. Blair
Craig Blower
Rudi M. Brewster
Sheldon I. Brockett, DDS
Carl R. Brown
Gerard J. Brown
James H. Buley
Mark S. Burgess
Dennis Burks
Malin Burnham
Lyle W. Butler
Steven E. Cairncross
Michelle Candland
Jack A. Carpenter
Samuel Carpenter

Edward R. Chaplin, MD

Charles H. Christian

Vincent R. Ciruzzi

Larry R. Clapper

Garet B. Clark

Nicole A. Clay

Mary G. Colacicco, PhD

H. Michael Collins

Barbara Cook

Richard D. Coutts, MD

Richard W. Cox

Tyler W. Cramer

Joseph W. Craver

Linda Crogan

Dean M. Crowder

Frederick P. Crowell

Jose G. da Rosa

Jack E. Damson

Michael G. Daniels

Darlene G. Davies

Daryl E. Day

Richard A. DeBolt

Arthur DeFever

Martha G. Dennis, PhD

Robert D. Dicioccio

Jan S. Driscoll

Charles W. Duddles

Berit N. Durler

Rodney R. Eales

Margaret F. Eddy

Marlee J. Ehrenfeld

Raymond G. Ellis

Peter K. Ellsworth

Craig S. Evanco

Daryl E. Ferguson

Thompson Fetter

Andrew Fichthorn

James Fitzpatrick

Robert C. Fletcher

C. F. Flynn

Howard B. Frank

Joan Friedenberg

Bruce H. Frost

Gordon T. Frost, Jr.

James R. Furby

Tom Gable

Joyce M. Gattas

Tom Gehring

Philip L. Gildred, Jr.

Edwin L. Glazener, MD

Joyce A. Glazer

James R. Goode

Ewart W. Goodwin, Jr.

William D. Gore

Gary G. Gould

Richard M. Green, DPM

James W. Groen

Roger W. Haines, Jr.

James M. Hall

Paul J. Hartley III

Albert T. Harutunian III

John S. Hattox, MD

James C. Haugh

William E. Hendrix, DDS

Daniel D. Herde

William M. Herrin,
    USMC (Ret.)

Andrew W. Hewitt

Sharon E. Hilliard

Joseph M. Horiye

Marie K. Huff

Darrell Hunsaker

Bruce A. Hunt

Karen Hutchens

Robert W. Hymes, DDS

David W. Jackson

James H. Jackson, Jr., PhD

Richard W. Jackson

Todd R. Jackson

Jo Dee C. Jacob

James C. Jessop

R. Bruce Johnson, MD

R. Kendal Jones

Morton C. Jorgensen, MD

Natasha Josefowitz, PhD

Mel I. Katz

Katherine Kennedy

Michael Kenny

Donald B. Kent

Henry M. Killmar

Russell W. Kirbey

Bill Kolender

Larry Kuntz

Robert C. Kyle

Sarah K. Lamade

Roy E. Lange

Thomas F. Larwin

Chester A. Lathrop

Nancy S. Laturno-Bojanic

Kimberley B. Layton

Cathleen LeClair

Richard S. Ledford

John Littrell

Gordon K. Lutes

Guy Maddox

Sandra L. Mayberry

Sandra L. McBrayer

Scott McClendon

Judith E. McDonald

William M. McKenzie, Jr.

Ray McKewon

Daniel G. McKinney

Laurence A. Miller, MD

Lisa S. Miller, MD

Neil Morgan

John L. Morrell

Michael A. Morton

Thomas F. Mosher, MD

Vincent E. Mudd

Edward C. Muns

Mike W. Murphy

Vincent Nares

Gary R. Nelson

Burton H. Nestor

Paul Nestor

William W. Newbern

Charles E. Nickel

Gregory V. Noonan

Kay G. North

David B. Oates

Stephen P. Oggel

Frank Panarisi

Leon W. Parma

Joanne Pastula

Douglas C. Paul

VAdm. R. E. Peet,
    USN (Ret.)

Gloria Penner

H. Newton Pollock

Ross M. Pyle

Donald G. Ramras, MD

John G. Rebelo, Jr.

John K. Reid

James O. Reynolds

Lawrence Richman

Garry Ridge

Arthur L. Rivkin

Patricia L. Roscoe

Michael S. Rowan

Eugene W. Rumsey, Jr., MD

Robert G. Russell, Jr.

Harold G. Sadler

Norbert Sanders

Eugene H. Sapper

G. Bradford Saunders

Donald L. Schoell

Larry G. Showley

Alvin J. Sibel

Christopher J. Sichel

Scott H. Silverman

Sidney R. Silverman

Michael J. Sise, MD

Sidney C. Smith, Jr., MD

Susan Snow

Suzanne Spafford

Cecil H. Steppe

Lawrence Stirling

Linda Stirling

Richard M. Sullivan, MD

Marc Tarasuck

Donald V. Tartre

Donald Teemsma, Jr.

M. Murray Tenney, Jr.

Robert C. Thaxton, Jr.

Mark C. Trotter

Jerald Van Ert

Thomas R. Vecchione, MD

Ramona Walker

Mary L. Walshok

Colin W. Wied

Cheryl Wilson

Thomas D. Wilson

Jean Young

Joseph A. Zakowski, DDS

Greg Zinser

John J. Zygowicz

Index

ROTARY CLUB 33 OF SAN DIEGO
ROTARY INTERNATIONAL
1911-2011 • 100 YEARS OF SERVICE

Ro
of S
100 y